BESTSELLERS John Sutherland
THE BIBLE John Riches
BIBLICAL ARCHAEOLOGY Eric H. Cline
BIOGRAPHY Hermione Lee
THE BLUES Elijah Wald
THE BOOK OF MORMON
    Terryl Givens
BORDERS Alexander C. Diener and
    Joshua Hagen
THE BRAIN Michael O'Shea
THE BRITISH CONSTITUTION
    Martin Loughlin
THE BRITISH EMPIRE Ashley Jackson
BRITISH POLITICS Anthony Wright
BUDDHA Michael Carrithers
BUDDHISM Damien Keown
BUDDHIST ETHICS Damien Keown
BYZANTIUM Peter Sarris
CANCER Nicholas James
CAPITALISM James Fulcher
CATHOLICISM Gerald O'Collins
CAUSATION Stephen Mumford and
    Rani Lill Anjum
THE CELL Terence Allen and
    Graham Cowling
THE CELTS Barry Cunliffe
CHAOS Leonard Smith
CHEMISTRY Peter Atkins
CHILD PSYCHOLOGY Usha Goswami
CHILDREN'S LITERATURE
    Kimberley Reynolds
CHINESE LITERATURE Sabina Knight
CHOICE THEORY Michael Allingham
CHRISTIAN ART Beth Williamson
CHRISTIAN ETHICS D. Stephen Long
CHRISTIANITY Linda Woodhead
CITIZENSHIP Richard Bellamy
CIVIL ENGINEERING David Muir Wood
CLASSICAL LITERATURE William Allan
CLASSICAL MYTHOLOGY
    Helen Morales
CLASSICS Mary Beard and John Henderson
CLAUSEWITZ Michael Howard
CLIMATE Mark Maslin
THE COLD WAR Robert McMahon
COLONIAL AMERICA Alan Taylor
COLONIAL LATIN AMERICAN
    LITERATURE Rolena Adorno
COMEDY Matthew Bevis
COMMUNISM Leslie Holmes
COMPLEXITY John H. Holland

THE COMPUTER Darrel Ince
CONFUCIANISM Daniel K. Gardner
THE CONQUISTADORS
    Matthew Restall and
    Felipe Fernández-Armesto
CONSCIENCE Paul Strohm
CONSCIOUSNESS Susan Blackmore
CONTEMPORARY ART Julian Stallabrass
CONTEMPORARY FICTION
    Robert Eaglestone
CONTINENTAL PHILOSOPHY
    Simon Critchley
CORAL REEFS Charles Sheppard
CORPORATE SOCIAL RESPONSIBILITY
    Jeremy Moon
CORRUPTION Leslie Holmes
COSMOLOGY Peter Coles
CRIME FICTION Richard Bradford
CRIMINAL JUSTICE Julian V. Roberts
CRITICAL THEORY Stephen Eric Bronner
THE CRUSADES Christopher Tyerman
CRYPTOGRAPHY Fred Piper and
    Sean Murphy
THE CULTURAL REVOLUTION
    Richard Curt Kraus
DADA AND SURREALISM
    David Hopkins
DANTE Peter Hainsworth and David Robey
DARWIN Jonathan Howard
THE DEAD SEA SCROLLS Timothy Lim
DEMOCRACY Bernard Crick
DERRIDA Simon Glendinning
DESCARTES Tom Sorell
DESERTS Nick Middleton
DESIGN John Heskett
DEVELOPMENTAL BIOLOGY
    Lewis Wolpert
THE DEVIL Darren Oldridge
DIASPORA Kevin Kenny
DICTIONARIES Lynda Mugglestone
DINOSAURS David Norman
DIPLOMACY Joseph M. Siracusa
DOCUMENTARY FILM
    Patricia Aufderheide
DREAMING J. Allan Hobson
DRUGS Leslie Iversen
DRUIDS Barry Cunliffe
EARLY MUSIC Thomas Forrest Kelly
THE EARTH Martin Redfern
ECONOMICS Partha Dasgupta
EDUCATION Gary Thomas

KT-219-976

EGYPTIAN MYTH Geraldine Pinch
EIGHTEENTH-CENTURY BRITAIN
    Paul Langford
THE ELEMENTS Philip Ball
EMOTION Dylan Evans
EMPIRE Stephen Howe
ENGELS Terrell Carver
ENGINEERING David Blockley
ENGLISH LITERATURE Jonathan Bate
THE ENLIGHTENMENT John Robertson
ENTREPRENEURSHIP Paul Westhead
    and Mike Wright
ENVIRONMENTAL ECONOMICS
    Stephen Smith
EPIDEMIOLOGY Rodolfo Saracci
ETHICS Simon Blackburn
ETHNOMUSICOLOGY Timothy Rice
THE ETRUSCANS Christopher Smith
THE EUROPEAN UNION John Pinder
    and Simon Usherwood
EVOLUTION Brian and
    Deborah Charlesworth
EXISTENTIALISM Thomas Flynn
EXPLORATION Stewart A. Weaver
THE EYE Michael Land
FAMILY LAW Jonathan Herring
FASCISM Kevin Passmore
FASHION Rebecca Arnold
FEMINISM Margaret Walters
FILM Michael Wood
FILM MUSIC Kathryn Kalinak
THE FIRST WORLD WAR
    Michael Howard
FOLK MUSIC Mark Slobin
FOOD John Krebs
FORENSIC PSYCHOLOGY David Canter
FORENSIC SCIENCE Jim Fraser
FORESTS Jaboury Ghazoul
FOSSILS Keith Thomson
FOUCAULT Gary Gutting
FRACTALS Kenneth Falconer
FREE SPEECH Nigel Warburton
FREE WILL Thomas Pink
FRENCH LITERATURE John D. Lyons
THE FRENCH REVOLUTION
    William Doyle
FREUD Anthony Storr
FUNDAMENTALISM Malise Ruthven
GALAXIES John Gribbin
GALILEO Stillman Drake

GAME THEORY Ken Binmore
GANDHI Bhikhu Parekh
GENES Jonathan Slack
GENIUS Andrew Robinson
GEOGRAPHY John Matthews and
    David Herbert
GEOPOLITICS Klaus Dodds
GERMAN LITERATURE Nicholas Boyle
GERMAN PHILOSOPHY Andrew Bowie
GLOBAL CATASTROPHES Bill McGuire
GLOBAL ECONOMIC HISTORY
    Robert C. Allen
GLOBALIZATION Manfred Steger
GOD John Bowker
THE GOTHIC Nick Groom
GOVERNANCE Mark Bevir
THE GREAT DEPRESSION AND
    THE NEW DEAL Eric Rauchway
HABERMAS James Gordon Finlayson
HAPPINESS Daniel M. Haybron
HEGEL Peter Singer
HEIDEGGER Michael Inwood
HERMENEUTICS Jens Zimmermann
HERODOTUS Jennifer T. Roberts
HIEROGLYPHS Penelope Wilson
HINDUISM Kim Knott
HISTORY John H. Arnold
THE HISTORY OF ASTRONOMY
    Michael Hoskin
THE HISTORY OF LIFE Michael Benton
THE HISTORY OF MATHEMATICS
    Jacqueline Stedall
THE HISTORY OF MEDICINE
    William Bynum
THE HISTORY OF TIME
    Leofranc Holford-Strevens
HIV/AIDS Alan Whiteside
HOBBES Richard Tuck
HORMONES Martin Luck
HUMAN ANATOMY Leslie Klenerman
HUMAN EVOLUTION Bernard Wood
HUMAN RIGHTS Andrew Clapham
HUMANISM Stephen Law
HUME A. J. Ayer
HUMOUR Noël Carroll
THE ICE AGE Jamie Woodward
IDEOLOGY Michael Freeden
INDIAN PHILOSOPHY Sue Hamilton
INFECTIOUS DISEASE Marta L. Wayne
    and Benjamin M. Bolker

Human Rights: A Very Short Introduction

VERY SHORT INTRODUCTIONS are for anyone wanting a stimulating and accessible way into a new subject. They are written by experts, and have been translated into more than 40 different languages.

The Series began in 1995, and now covers a wide variety of topics in every discipline. The VSI library now contains over 450 volumes—a Very Short Introduction to everything from Psychology and Philosophy of Science to American History and Relativity—and continues to grow in every subject area.

Very Short Introductions available now:

ACCOUNTING Christopher Nobes
ADVERTISING Winston Fletcher
AFRICAN AMERICAN RELIGION
    Eddie S. Glaude Jr.
AFRICAN HISTORY John Parker and
    Richard Rathbone
AFRICAN RELIGIONS Jacob K. Olupona
AGNOSTICISM Robin Le Poidevin
ALEXANDER THE GREAT Hugh Bowden
ALGEBRA Peter M. Higgins
AMERICAN HISTORY Paul S. Boyer
AMERICAN IMMIGRATION
    David A. Gerber
AMERICAN LEGAL HISTORY
    G. Edward White
AMERICAN POLITICAL HISTORY
    Donald Critchlow
AMERICAN POLITICAL PARTIES
    AND ELECTIONS L. Sandy Maisel
AMERICAN POLITICS Richard M. Valelly
THE AMERICAN PRESIDENCY
    Charles O. Jones
THE AMERICAN REVOLUTION
    Robert J. Allison
AMERICAN SLAVERY
    Heather Andrea Williams
THE AMERICAN WEST Stephen Aron
AMERICAN WOMEN'S HISTORY
    Susan Ware
ANAESTHESIA Aidan O'Donnell
ANARCHISM Colin Ward
ANCIENT ASSYRIA Karen Radner
ANCIENT EGYPT Ian Shaw
ANCIENT EGYPTIAN ART AND
    ARCHITECTURE Christina Riggs

ANCIENT GREECE Paul Cartledge
THE ANCIENT NEAR EAST
    Amanda H. Podany
ANCIENT PHILOSOPHY Julia Annas
ANCIENT WARFARE
    Harry Sidebottom
ANGELS David Albert Jones
ANGLICANISM Mark Chapman
THE ANGLO-SAXON AGE John Blair
THE ANIMAL KINGDOM
    Peter Holland
ANIMAL RIGHTS David DeGrazia
THE ANTARCTIC Klaus Dodds
ANTISEMITISM Steven Beller
ANXIETY Daniel Freeman and
    Jason Freeman
THE APOCRYPHAL GOSPELS
    Paul Foster
ARCHAEOLOGY Paul Bahn
ARCHITECTURE Andrew Ballantyne
ARISTOCRACY William Doyle
ARISTOTLE Jonathan Barnes
ART HISTORY Dana Arnold
ART THEORY Cynthia Freeland
ASTROBIOLOGY David C. Catling
ATHEISM Julian Baggini
AUGUSTINE Henry Chadwick
AUSTRALIA Kenneth Morgan
AUTISM Uta Frith
THE AVANT GARDE David Cottington
THE AZTECS David Carrasco
BACTERIA Sebastian G. B. Amyes
BARTHES Jonathan Culler
THE BEATS David Sterritt
BEAUTY Roger Scruton

INFORMATION Luciano Floridi
INNOVATION Mark Dodgson and David Gann
INTELLIGENCE Ian J. Deary
INTERNATIONAL MIGRATION Khalid Koser
INTERNATIONAL RELATIONS Paul Wilkinson
INTERNATIONAL SECURITY Christopher S. Browning
IRAN Ali M. Ansari
ISLAM Malise Ruthven
ISLAMIC HISTORY Adam Silverstein
ITALIAN LITERATURE Peter Hainsworth and David Robey
JESUS Richard Bauckham
JOURNALISM Ian Hargreaves
JUDAISM Norman Solomon
JUNG Anthony Stevens
KABBALAH Joseph Dan
KAFKA Ritchie Robertson
KANT Roger Scruton
KEYNES Robert Skidelsky
KIERKEGAARD Patrick Gardiner
KNOWLEDGE Jennifer Nagel
THE KORAN Michael Cook
LANDSCAPE ARCHITECTURE Ian H. Thompson
LANDSCAPES AND GEOMORPHOLOGY Andrew Goudie and Heather Viles
LANGUAGES Stephen R. Anderson
LATE ANTIQUITY Gillian Clark
LAW Raymond Wacks
THE LAWS OF THERMODYNAMICS Peter Atkins
LEADERSHIP Keith Grint
LIBERALISM Michael Freeden
LIGHT Ian Walmsley
LINCOLN Allen C. Guelzo
LINGUISTICS Peter Matthews
LITERARY THEORY Jonathan Culler
LOCKE John Dunn
LOGIC Graham Priest
LOVE Ronald de Sousa
MACHIAVELLI Quentin Skinner
MADNESS Andrew Scull
MAGIC Owen Davies
MAGNA CARTA Nicholas Vincent
MAGNETISM Stephen Blundell
MALTHUS Donald Winch
MANAGEMENT John Hendry
MAO Delia Davin
MARINE BIOLOGY Philip V. Mladenov
THE MARQUIS DE SADE John Phillips
MARTIN LUTHER Scott H. Hendrix
MARTYRDOM Jolyon Mitchell
MARX Peter Singer
MATERIALS Christopher Hall
MATHEMATICS Timothy Gowers
THE MEANING OF LIFE Terry Eagleton
MEDICAL ETHICS Tony Hope
MEDICAL LAW Charles Foster
MEDIEVAL BRITAIN John Gillingham and Ralph A. Griffiths
MEDIEVAL LITERATURE Elaine Treharne
MEMORY Jonathan K. Foster
METAPHYSICS Stephen Mumford
MICHAEL FARADAY Frank A. J. L. James
MICROBIOLOGY Nicholas P. Money
MICROECONOMICS Avinash Dixit
MICROSCOPY Terence Allen
THE MIDDLE AGES Miri Rubin
MINERALS David Vaughan
MODERN ART David Cottington
MODERN CHINA Rana Mitter
MODERN FRANCE Vanessa R. Schwartz
MODERN IRELAND Senia Pašeta
MODERN JAPAN Christopher Goto-Jones
MODERN LATIN AMERICAN LITERATURE Roberto González Echevarría
MODERN WAR Richard English
MODERNISM Christopher Butler
MOLECULES Philip Ball
THE MONGOLS Morris Rossabi
MORMONISM Richard Lyman Bushman
MOUNTAINS Martin F. Price
MUHAMMAD Jonathan A. C. Brown
MULTICULTURALISM Ali Rattansi
MUSIC Nicholas Cook
MYTH Robert A. Segal
THE NAPOLEONIC WARS Mike Rapport
NATIONALISM Steven Grosby
NELSON MANDELA Elleke Boehmer
NEOLIBERALISM Manfred Steger and Ravi Roy

NETWORKS Guido Caldarelli and
    Michele Catanzaro
THE NEW TESTAMENT
    Luke Timothy Johnson
THE NEW TESTAMENT AS
    LITERATURE Kyle Keefer
NEWTON Robert Iliffe
NIETZSCHE Michael Tanner
NINETEENTH-CENTURY BRITAIN
    Christopher Harvie and
    H. C. G. Matthew
THE NORMAN CONQUEST
    George Garnett
NORTH AMERICAN INDIANS
    Theda Perdue and Michael D. Green
NORTHERN IRELAND
    Marc Mulholland
NOTHING Frank Close
NUCLEAR PHYSICS Frank Close
NUCLEAR POWER Maxwell Irvine
NUCLEAR WEAPONS Joseph M. Siracusa
NUMBERS Peter M. Higgins
NUTRITION David A. Bender
OBJECTIVITY Stephen Gaukroger
THE OLD TESTAMENT
    Michael D. Coogan
THE ORCHESTRA D. Kern Holoman
ORGANIZATIONS Mary Jo Hatch
PAGANISM Owen Davies
THE PALESTINIAN-ISRAELI
    CONFLICT Martin Bunton
PARTICLE PHYSICS Frank Close
PAUL E. P. Sanders
PEACE Oliver P. Richmond
PENTECOSTALISM William K. Kay
THE PERIODIC TABLE Eric R. Scerri
PHILOSOPHY Edward Craig
PHILOSOPHY IN THE ISLAMIC
    WORLD Peter Adamson
PHILOSOPHY OF LAW
    Raymond Wacks
PHILOSOPHY OF SCIENCE
    Samir Okasha
PHOTOGRAPHY Steve Edwards
PHYSICAL CHEMISTRY Peter Atkins
PILGRIMAGE Ian Reader
PLAGUE Paul Slack
PLANETS David A. Rothery
PLANTS Timothy Walker
PLATE TECTONICS Peter Molnar
PLATO Julia Annas

POLITICAL PHILOSOPHY David Miller
POLITICS Kenneth Minogue
POSTCOLONIALISM Robert Young
POSTMODERNISM Christopher Butler
POSTSTRUCTURALISM
    Catherine Belsey
PREHISTORY Chris Gosden
PRESOCRATIC PHILOSOPHY
    Catherine Osborne
PRIVACY Raymond Wacks
PROBABILITY John Haigh
PROGRESSIVISM Walter Nugent
PROTESTANTISM Mark A. Noll
PSYCHIATRY Tom Burns
PSYCHOANALYSIS Daniel Pick
PSYCHOLOGY Gillian Butler and
    Freda McManus
PSYCHOTHERAPY Tom Burns and
    Eva Burns-Lundgren
PURITANISM Francis J. Bremer
THE QUAKERS Pink Dandelion
QUANTUM THEORY
    John Polkinghorne
RACISM Ali Rattansi
RADIOACTIVITY Claudio Tuniz
RASTAFARI Ennis B. Edmonds
THE REAGAN REVOLUTION Gil Troy
REALITY Jan Westerhoff
THE REFORMATION Peter Marshall
RELATIVITY Russell Stannard
RELIGION IN AMERICA Timothy Beal
THE RENAISSANCE Jerry Brotton
RENAISSANCE ART
    Geraldine A. Johnson
REVOLUTIONS Jack A. Goldstone
RHETORIC Richard Toye
RISK Baruch Fischhoff and John Kadvany
RITUAL Barry Stephenson
RIVERS Nick Middleton
ROBOTICS Alan Winfield
ROMAN BRITAIN Peter Salway
THE ROMAN EMPIRE Christopher Kelly
THE ROMAN REPUBLIC
    David M. Gwynn
ROMANTICISM Michael Ferber
ROUSSEAU Robert Wokler
RUSSELL A. C. Grayling
RUSSIAN HISTORY Geoffrey Hosking
RUSSIAN LITERATURE Catriona Kelly
THE RUSSIAN REVOLUTION
    S. A. Smith

SCHIZOPHRENIA Chris Frith and
    Eve Johnstone
SCHOPENHAUER
    Christopher Janaway
SCIENCE AND RELIGION
    Thomas Dixon
SCIENCE FICTION David Seed
THE SCIENTIFIC REVOLUTION
    Lawrence M. Principe
SCOTLAND Rab Houston
SEXUALITY Véronique Mottier
SIKHISM Eleanor Nesbitt
THE SILK ROAD James A. Millward
SLEEP Steven W. Lockley and
    Russell G. Foster
SOCIAL AND CULTURAL
    ANTHROPOLOGY
    John Monaghan and Peter Just
SOCIAL PSYCHOLOGY
    Richard J. Crisp
SOCIAL WORK Sally Holland and
    Jonathan Scourfield
SOCIALISM Michael Newman
SOCIOLINGUISTICS John Edwards
SOCIOLOGY Steve Bruce
SOCRATES C. C. W. Taylor
THE SOVIET UNION Stephen Lovell
THE SPANISH CIVIL WAR
    Helen Graham
SPANISH LITERATURE Jo Labanyi
SPINOZA Roger Scruton
SPIRITUALITY Philip Sheldrake
SPORT Mike Cronin
STARS Andrew King
STATISTICS David J. Hand
STEM CELLS Jonathan Slack
STRUCTURAL ENGINEERING
    David Blockley
STUART BRITAIN John Morrill

SUPERCONDUCTIVITY
    Stephen Blundell
SYMMETRY Ian Stewart
TAXATION Stephen Smith
TEETH Peter S. Ungar
TERRORISM Charles Townshend
THEATRE Marvin Carlson
THEOLOGY David F. Ford
THOMAS AQUINAS Fergus Kerr
THOUGHT Tim Bayne
TIBETAN BUDDHISM
    Matthew T. Kapstein
TOCQUEVILLE Harvey C. Mansfield
TRAGEDY Adrian Poole
THE TROJAN WAR Eric H. Cline
TRUST Katherine Hawley
THE TUDORS John Guy
TWENTIETH-CENTURY BRITAIN
    Kenneth O. Morgan
THE UNITED NATIONS
    Jussi M. Hanhimäki
THE U.S. CONGRESS Donald A. Ritchie
THE U.S. SUPREME COURT
    Linda Greenhouse
UTOPIANISM Lyman Tower Sargent
THE VIKINGS Julian Richards
VIRUSES Dorothy H. Crawford
WATER John Finney
WILLIAM SHAKESPEARE
    Stanley Wells
WITCHCRAFT Malcolm Gaskill
WITTGENSTEIN A. C. Grayling
WORK Stephen Fineman
WORLD MUSIC Philip Bohlman
THE WORLD TRADE ORGANIZATION
    Amrita Narlikar
WORLD WAR II Gerhard L. Weinberg
WRITING AND SCRIPT
    Andrew Robinson

Available soon:

BLACK HOLES Katherine Blundell
INTERNATIONAL LAW
    Vaughan Lowe

SOUND Mike Goldsmith
EPICUREANISM Catherine Wilson
MOONS David A. Rothery

For more information visit our website

www.oup.com/vsi/

Andrew Clapham

HUMAN RIGHTS

A Very Short Introduction
SECOND EDITION

OXFORD
UNIVERSITY PRESS

OXFORD
UNIVERSITY PRESS

Great Clarendon Street, Oxford, OX2 6DP,
United Kingdom

Oxford University Press is a department of the University of Oxford.
It furthers the University's objective of excellence in research, scholarship,
and education by publishing worldwide. Oxford is a registered trade mark of
Oxford University Press in the UK and in certain other countries

First edition published in 2007
Second edition published in 2015

Impression: 5

Published in the United States of America by Oxford University Press
198 Madison Avenue, New York, NY 10016, United States of America

British Library Cataloguing in Publication Data

Data available

Library of Congress Control Number: 2015941392

ISBN 978–0–19–870616–8

Printed in Great Britain by
Ashford Colour Press Ltd, Gosport, Hampshire

Contents

Preface xiii

Acknowledgements xv

List of illustrations xvii

1 Looking at rights 1

2 Historical development and contemporary concerns 27

3 Human rights foreign policy and the role of the United Nations 63

4 Torture 83

5 Deprivations of life and liberty 98

6 Balancing rights—free speech and privacy 110

7 Food, education, health, housing, and work 122

8 Discrimination and equality 140

9 The death penalty 153

Final remarks 161

Publisher's acknowledgements 167

References 169

Further reading 179

Annex: The Universal Declaration of Human Rights 185

Index 193

Human Rights

Preface

The aim of this book is to provide the reader with some entry points into the worlds of human rights thinking, activism, and law. This book concentrates on the power of ideas to mobilize people against injustice and indignities. Human rights do not really resolve the tension between competing interests and various visions of how the world should be; rather, human rights ideas provide a vocabulary for arguing about which interests should prevail and how to create the conditions for constraining attacks on dignity.

This short introduction focuses on the content of a number of rights rather than simply telling the human rights story of revolutions, proclamations, and continuing struggles. Calling for a world based on respect for human rights is easy; adjusting current arrangements to achieve full respect for human rights is a never-ending process, even more difficult when we consider that human rights are not just an ideal, but actually consist of concrete rights to life, liberty, equality, free speech, privacy, health, food, and housing. Human rights are about each of us living in dignity, and we are a long way from achieving that on a global scale. We shall see that the human rights project is not simply about implementing a set of obligations fixed in history; rather, the human rights movement is about people standing up to injustice and showing solidarity in the face of oppression.

In order to allow readers to discover for themselves some of the texts and organizations referred to in this introduction there is an accompanying website: <http://graduateinstitute.ch/clapham-humanrights>, the full text of most references can be found on this website.

Acknowledgements

I should like to thank all those at Oxford University Press who worked to bring this project to fruition. Special thanks go to Emma Ma, Andrea Keegan, Jenny Nugee, Mohana Annamalai, Joy Mellor, Ruby Constable, and Sophie Basilevitch, as well as to the anonymous reviewers whose very helpful comments have improved the text.

Here at the Graduate Institute of International and Development Studies in Geneva, and at the Geneva Academy of International Humanitarian Law and Human Rights I have been fortunate to have excellent graduate students, who have asked hard questions and kept me on my toes. I should like to thank to Oana Ichim for her help on the cases, and I am very grateful indeed for the painstaking work done by Ilia Siatitsa both on the text and in preparing the documents that are posted on the companion website.

Lastly, let me express my gratitude to two people from my family: my mother, Margaret Clapham, who provides a press-cuttings service second to none and nourished the project, and my wife, Mona Rishmawi, whose own work for human rights is a daily reminder that the human rights story is not only about past texts, but also about daily struggles in the face of discrimination, oppression, and brutality.

A.B.C.
Graduate Institute of International and Development Studies, Geneva

List of illustrations

1 'Criminals' Rights Act' **2**
© Telegraph Media Group Limited
2006

2 Mary Wollstonecraft **11**
The Bodleian Library, University of
Oxford, (OC) 210 m. 460

3 *Rights of Man* book cover **36**
(c) Penguin Books

4 George Washington
Williams **40**
Library of Congress

5 Radislav Krstić: before and
after images **44**
Michel Porro/Getty Images, and
© Reuters/Ranko Cukovic

6 Child soldiers in the
Democratic Republic of
Congo **47**
© Roger LeMoyne

7 Demonstration in Berne **69**
© Amnesty International (Suisse)
2003

8 Mothers of the 'disappeared',
Buenos Aires **73**
Rafael Wollmann/Gamma-Rapho via
Getty Images

9 ISIS execution **77**
AFP Photo/Ho/Welayat
Salahuddin

10 Human Rights Council voting
on the Sri Lanka Resolution
2014 **78**
UN Photo/Jean-Marc Ferré

11 'Resign, Rumsfeld': front
cover of *The Economist*, 8 May
2004 **87**
© *The Economist*

12 The Appeal for Amnesty,
28 May 1961 **105**
Copyright Guardian News & Media
Ltd 1961

13 Patrick Stewart on domestic
violence, Amnesty
magazine **149**
© Amnesty International UK

14 Guantánamo war crimes
   trial before the Military
   Commission 2014,
   sketch **158**
   © Janet Hamlin

15 a. Modern lethal injection
   apparatus; and b. the
   guillotine **159**
   a. William F. Campbell/Time Life
   Images Collection/Getty Images; and
   b. Popperfoto/Getty Images

Chapter 1
Looking at rights

These days it is usually not long before a problem is expressed as a human rights issue. This book looks at where the concept of human rights came from and how the human rights movement has developed a set of obligations that apply worldwide. We will consider the trajectory of the idea of human rights and the role that human rights play (and might come to play) in our world.

Different people currently see human rights in different ways. For some, invoking human rights is a heartfelt, morally justified demand to rectify all sorts of injustice; for others, it is no more than a slogan to be treated with suspicion, or even hostility. Lawyers sometimes consider that human rights represent almost a term of art, representing only those claims that have been or can be upheld as legal rights by a national or international court. Yet the application of human rights law in court is almost always contested, with both parties to a dispute demanding that human rights law be applied in their favour. Human rights law is special and popular as it often suggests that other law is inadequate or applied in an unfair way. The language of human rights is deployed to criticize, defend, and reform all sorts of behaviour. Human rights have a pedigree of a distinguished struggle against oppression and the promise of a fairer future. Playing the 'human rights card' can be persuasive, sometimes even conclusive, in contemporary decision making; this is one aspect of what makes the moral force of human rights so attractive—human rights help you to win arguments and, sometimes, to change the way things are done.

The concept of a 'human rights culture' also means different things to different people. To some, it means ensuring that everyone is treated with respect for their inherent dignity and human worth. To others, it means that judges, the police, and immigration officials are required to protect the interests of terrorists, criminals, and migrants at the expense of the security of the population (see Figure 1). This tension has come to a head in some countries, including the United Kingdom, with popular newspapers ridiculing the application of human rights legislation (see Box 1) and campaigning against the role of 'foreign judges'.

At times, human rights protections may indeed seem to be anti-majoritarian; why should judges or international bodies determine what is best for any society, especially when democratically elected representatives have chosen a particular path? But the point is that human rights may serve to protect

1. Headline from *The Sunday Telegraph*, 14 May 2006: branding the Human Rights Act 'the refuge of terrorists and scoundrels'.

Box 1 Human rights and the British backlash

Chris Grayling MP, in the *Daily Mail* (2014), 'We must seize power from Euro judges and return the phrase Human Rights to what it really should be—a symbol of the fight against oppression and brutality'

'Prisoners being allowed artificial insemination treatment in order to protect their family rights, votes for prisoners in our jails, no whole-life sentences for the most brutal murderers, no deportation for terrorists—some of the decisions that the European Court of Human Rights has taken in recent years—and we came within one vote from one judge of being required to permit US style political TV advertising.

These are not great principles of human rights. They are decisions taken by a Court, made up of people who are not by any means all legally qualified, that sees the original European Convention as a "living instrument", to be rewritten as the years go by. All of them should be matters for our Parliament and not for the Courts to decide. But right now they aren't.

Quite simply, that is not what we signed up to. So the next Conservative Government will sort this out once and for all.

We won't walk away from the principles of human rights. But we will say very clearly that we are a sovereign nation, which upholds the best of human rights, and that decisions about our nation should be taken by our Parliament.'

Susan Marks (2014), *Backlash: The Undeclared War against Human Rights.*

'There is the same kind of reactive assault that Faludi described in her account of the backlash against women's rights in America. It is the (likewise limited) gains of the human rights movement that are now to be rolled back. There is the same pattern whereby, in our case, human rights are blamed for

3

people from the 'tyranny of the majority'. Human rights law, however,
should not be seen as a simple device to thwart the wishes of the
majority, as, with the exception of the absolute ban on torture, it
does in fact allow for security needs and the rights of others to
be taken into consideration in a democratic society. There is no
easy answer to this conundrum that asks why judges should
be entitled to uphold human rights in the face of democratic
decisions. Different societies will choose different arrangements,
some will place more power in the hands of judges than others.
These arrangements may change over time—there is no perfect
balance; there is no perfect judge. Sometimes judges may be
seen by some as able to rein in a government that unjustifiably
tramples human rights, but that same judgment may be seen by
others as upholding the rights of property owners or employers
at the expense of a popular legislature mandated to protect
vulnerable workers or racial groups. Arguing about rights is a way
to argue about what sort of society we want. Rights to freedom of
expression and information can be useful in ensuring that we have
full democratic decision-making, and the same human rights can
also be used to challenge the resulting legislation. Whether those
claiming rights are actually right is something which we can only
know in context. So let us try to be a bit more concrete.

We first need to understand that *human rights* are a special,
narrow category of rights. William Edmundson's introductory

book on rights distinguishes human rights from other rights by suggesting that: 'Human rights recognize *extraordinarily* special, basic interests, and this sets them apart from rights, even moral rights, generally.' Richard Falk suggests that human rights are a 'new type of rights' achieving prominence as a result of the adoption of the Universal Declaration of Human Rights by the United Nations in 1948. This point is worth remembering throughout the book: we are not talking about all the rights that human beings may have—we are considering a rather special category of rights. The elevation of human rights to the international level after the Second World War has meant that behaviour can be judged, not only against what national law requires, but also against a standard which sits outside a national system. Every nation state is now subject to this scrutiny from outside.

Many who approach the subject of human rights turn to early religious and philosophical writings. In their vision of human rights, human beings are endowed, by reason of their humanity, with certain fundamental and inalienable rights. This conclusion has existed in various forms in various societies. The historic development of the concept of human rights is often also associated with the evolution of Western philosophical and political principles; yet a different perspective could find reference to similar principles concerning mass education, self-fulfilment, respect for others, and the quest to contribute to others' well-being in Confucian, Hindu, or Buddhist traditions. Religious texts such as the Bible and the Koran can be read as creating not only duties but also rights. Recognition of the need to protect human freedom and human dignity is alluded to in some of the earliest codes, from Hammurabi's Code in ancient Babylon (around 1780 BCE), right through to the natural law traditions of the West, which built on the Greek Stoics and the Roman law notion of *jus gentium* (law for all peoples). Common to each of these codes is the recognition of certain universally valid principles and standards of behaviour. These behavioural standards arguably inspire human rights thinking, and may be seen as precursors to, or different expressions of, the idea of human rights—but the lineage is not as obvious as is sometimes suggested. Let us now look at some early historical invocations of the actual concept of *rights* (as opposed to decent behaviour) and the sceptical responses they evoked.

The rights of man and their discontents

The standard Western account of the tradition of human rights is somewhat problematic. Early legal developments in the area of human rights are said to have emerged from the *Magna Carta* of 1215, a contract between the English King John and the Barons who were dissatisfied with the taxes being levied by the monarch. But, although this agreement guaranteed rights for a *freeman* not to be 'arrested, or detained in prison, or deprived of his freehold, or outlawed, or banished, or in any way molested...unless by lawful judgment of his peers and the law of the land', this guarantee was simply a right to trial by jury granted exclusively to property-owning men. The rights contained in the *Magna Carta* were part of a political settlement to entrench liberties of the governed and limit the powers of the government. Human rights, as that term is understood today, belong to all human beings and therefore cannot be restricted to a select group of privileged men. From a contemporary perspective, the *Magna Carta* cannot really be seen as an exemplary human rights declaration. Suffice it to cite one sentence, clause 54 of the *Magna Carta* reads: 'No one shall be arrested or imprisoned on the appeal of a woman for the death of any person except her husband.'

The *English Bill of Rights* of 1689 is similarly sometimes considered a stepping stone to today's texts. It declared that 'excessive bail ought not to be required, nor excessive fines imposed, nor cruel and unusual punishments inflicted'. It also declared, however, 'That the subjects which are Protestants, may have arms for their defence suitable to their conditions, and as allowed by law.' The *Bill of Rights* was developed by Parliament as a

Declaration of Rights in response to the ideas and policies of King James II (who was perceived to be altering the nature of the state and introducing too much tolerance for Catholicism), and presented to the incoming Joint Sovereigns William and Mary as a condition for their accession to the throne in order to vindicate 'ancient rights and liberties', protect freedom of speech, and limit interference by the Sovereign in Parliament and elections.

At the same time, the work of a number of philosophers had a very concrete influence on the articulation of demands in the form of 'natural rights' or the 'rights of man'. John Locke's *Second Treatise of Government*, published in 1690, considered men in a 'state of nature' where they enjoyed 'a state of liberty', yet it was not 'a state of licence'. Locke reasoned that everyone 'is bound to preserve himself' so when his own preservation is not threatened everyone should 'as much as he can . . . preserve the rest of mankind', and no one may 'take away or impair the life, or what tends to the preservation of the life, the liberty, health, limb, or goods of another'. In this way, 'men may be restrained from invading others' rights and from doing hurt to one another'. Locke saw civil government as the remedy for men acting as their own judges to enforce the law of nature. He considered that this social contract, freely entered into, entitled the government to enforce laws for as long as the government respected the trust placed in it. Should the people be subject to the exercise by the government of arbitrary or absolute power over their 'lives, liberties, and estates' then, according to Locke, governmental power would be forfeited and devolve back to the people.

The Social Contract of Jean-Jacques Rousseau developed the idea that an individual may have a private will (*volonté particulière*) and that his private interest (*intérêt particulier*) 'may dictate to him very differently from the common interest'. Rousseau considered that 'whoever refuses to obey the general will shall be

7

compelled to it by the whole body: this in fact only forces him to be free'. For Rousseau: 'Man loses by the social contract his *natural* liberty, and an unlimited right to all which tempts him, and which he can obtain; in return he acquires *civil* liberty, and proprietorship of all he possess.' Published in 1762, *The Social Contract* was a precursor to the French Revolution of 1789 and the ideas it expressed have had considerable influence around the world as people have sought to articulate the rights of the governors and the governed.

Thomas Paine was a radical English writer who participated in the revolutionary changes affecting America. He emigrated to America in 1774, and in 1776 produced a widely read pamphlet called *Common Sense* which attacked the idea of rule by monarchy and called for republican government and equal rights among citizens. He also worked on the 1776 Constitution of Pennsylvania and for the subsequent abolition of slavery in that state. Paine's publication, entitled *Rights of Man*, appeared in 1791 as a defence of the French Revolution in response to Edmund Burke's *Reflections on the Revolution in France*. Paine was popular with the people (one estimate suggests that various versions of *Rights of Man* sold 250,000 copies in two years). He was unpopular with the government and was convicted in his absence of seditious libel at the Guildhall in London. The crowds flocked to support his defence counsel, protesting the trampling of the 'liberty of the press'. Paine had by then already escaped to France and was rewarded with election to the National Convention for his defence of the Revolution. He was, however, later imprisoned, having angered the Jacobins for opposing the execution of the King. He himself escaped the death penalty (according to some accounts, the chalk mark was put on the wrong side of the door) and later left for America, where he died unfêted in 1809. His writings still resonate, and one does not have to look far to find bumper stickers and badges with Paine's aphorism from his *Rights of Man*: 'my country is the world, and my religion is to do good'.

Reading Paine reveals what it is that makes human rights such an enduring concept. Paine is sentimental about other people's suffering:

> When I contemplate the natural dignity of man; when I feel (for nature has not been kind enough to me to blunt my feelings) for the honour and happiness of its character, I become irritated at the attempt to govern mankind by force and fraud, as if they were all knaves and fools, and can scarcely avoid the disgust at those who are imposed upon.

Paine railed against Burke for failing to feel any compassion for those who had suffered in the Bastille prison and for being unaffected by the 'reality of distress'. We can see here, I would suggest, the real seeds of the human rights movement: a feeling of sympathy for the distress of others, coupled with a sense of injustice when governments resort to measures which invade the perceived natural rights of the individual.

The modern concept of human rights is thus traditionally easily traced to these ideas and texts adopted at the end of the 18th century. It is well known that the 1776 American Declaration of Independence stated: 'We hold these truths to be self-evident, that all men are created equal; that they are endowed by their Creator with certain unalienable rights; that among these are life, liberty and the pursuit of happiness.' The French *Declaration of the Rights of Man and of the Citizen* followed in 1789, and its familiar first two articles recognized and proclaimed that 'Men are born and remain free and equal in rights' and that 'The aim of every political association is the preservation of the natural and inalienable rights of man; these rights are liberty, property, security, and resistance to oppression.' Still, the rights they referred to were mostly relevant only to those states in relation to their citizens, and only specific groups could benefit from their protection. These revolutionary Declarations represent attempts to enshrine human rights as guiding principles in the constitutions of new states or polities. The Declarations were inspired by a liberal conception of society and a belief in natural law, human reason, and universal order. Rights were believed (by men) to be the exclusive property of those possessing the capacity to exercise rational choice (a group that excluded women). Attempts by Olympe de Gouge to promote (by appealing to Queen Marie Antoinette) a *Declaration of the Rights of Women* and a 'Social Contract Between Man and Woman', regulating property and inheritance rights, fell on deaf ears. In England, Mary Wollstonecraft's *Vindication of the Rights of Woman* appealed for a revision of the French Constitution to respect the rights of women, arguing that men could not decide for themselves what they judged would be best for women (see Figure 2). The denial of women's rights condemned women to the sphere of their families and left them 'groping in the dark' (see Box 2).

Box 2 Mary Wollstonecraft's dedication to Monsieur Talleyrand-Périgord in *A Vindication of the Rights of Women* (1792)

Consider—I address you as a legislator—whether, when men contend for their freedom, and to be allowed to judge for themselves respecting their own happiness, it be not inconsistent and unjust to subjugate women, even though you firmly believe that you are acting in the manner best calculated to promote their happiness? Who made man the exclusive judge, if women partake with him, the gift of reason? In this style argue tyrants of every denomination, from the weak king to the weak father of a family; they are all eager to crush reason, yet always assert that they usurp its throne only to be useful. Do you not act a similar part when you *force* all women, by denying them civil and political rights, to remain immured in their families groping in the dark? For surely, sir, you will not assert that a duty can be binding which is not founded on reason?

Opie pinx[t]   *Heath Sculp[t]*

Mary Wollstonecraft Godwin.

London, Published Jan.[y] 1.st 1798, by J. Johnson, S.[t] Pauls Church Yard.

2. Mary Wollstonecraft.

Karl Marx responded to the proclamation of rights in the Constitutions of Pennsylvania and New Hampshire and in the French Declaration by deriding the idea that rights could be useful in creating a new political community. For Marx, these rights stressed the individual's egoistic preoccupations, rather than providing human emancipation from religion, property, and law. Marx had a vision of a future community in which all needs would be satisfied, and in which there would be no conflicts of interests and, therefore, no role for rights or their enforcement. Marx also highlighted the puzzle that if rights can be limited for the public good then the proclamation that the aim of political life is the protection of rights becomes convoluted (see Box 3).

Box 3 Karl Marx, *On the Jewish Question* (1843)

It is puzzling enough that a people which is just beginning to liberate itself, to tear down all the barriers between its various sections, and to establish a political community, that such a people solemnly proclaims (Declaration of 1791) the rights of egoistic man separated from his fellow men and from the community, and that indeed it repeats this proclamation at a moment when only the most heroic devotion can save the nation, and is therefore imperatively called for, at a moment when the sacrifice of all the interests of civil society must be the order of the day, and egoism must be punished as a crime. (Declaration of the Rights of Man, etc., of 1793.) This fact becomes still more puzzling when we see that the political emancipators go so far as to reduce citizenship, and the *political community*, to a mere *means* for maintaining these so-called rights of man, that therefore the *citoyen* is declared to be the servant of egoistic *homme*, that the sphere in which man acts as a communal being is degraded to a level below the sphere in which he acts as a partial being, and that, finally, it is not man as *citoyen*, but man as *bourgeois* who is considered to be the *essential* and *true* man.

In the 19th century, natural rights, or the 'rights of man', became less relevant to political change, and thinkers such as Jeremy Bentham ridiculed the idea that 'All men are born free' as 'Absurd and miserable nonsense'. Bentham famously dismissed natural and imprescriptable rights as 'nonsense upon stilts', declaring that wanting something is not the same as having it. In Bentham's terms: 'hunger is not bread'. For Bentham, real rights were legal rights, and it was the role of law makers, and not natural rights advocates, to generate rights and determine their limits. Bentham considered that one was asking for trouble, inviting anarchy even, to suggest that government was constrained by natural rights.

The contemporary scholar Amartya Sen has recalled Bentham's influence, and highlighted a 'legitimacy critique' whereby some see human rights as 'pre-legal moral claims' that 'can hardly be seen as giving justiciable rights in courts and other institutions of enforcement'. Sen cautions against confusing human rights with 'legislated legal rights'. He also points to a further reaction to human rights discourse: it has been claimed by some that human rights are alien to some cultures which may prefer to prioritize other principles, such as respect for authority. Sen calls this the 'cultural critique'. This last criticism is a common preoccupation of commentators whenever the topic of human rights is raised. Indeed, *The Very Short Introduction to Empire* suggests that, for some observers, the International Criminal Tribunal for the former Yugoslavia (well known for the aborted trial of Slobodan Milošović) is an imperialist creation, and that for 'such critics, the whole idea of "universal" human rights is actually a gigantic fraud, where Western imperialist or ex-colonial powers try to pass off their own, very specific and localized, idea of what "rights" should be as universal, trampling roughly over everyone else's beliefs and traditions'.

We can respond to such criticism as follows. First, while Bentham was right that natural rights had no agreed content or legal legitimacy at that time, today such rights have been given content and agreed to by legislatures and governments. There is no state in the world that has not agreed to abide by at least one human rights treaty. Secondly, the type of rights being promoted abroad is not as alien as is sometimes claimed. Today, although some leaders might seek to brush off human rights criticism as alien or Western, it is more likely that rights will be claimed from the bottom-up as part of a campaign to protest against oppression, than human rights will be raised in a hectoring way in a summit between leaders. All this does not mean that there is no room for different cultures to choose different outcomes when rights collide. As we shall see, the modern catalogue of human rights allows for most rights to be limited in order to take into account the rights of others.

Some will say we have still not really proven that these rights exist, beyond laws and treaties, as a question of moral logic for everyone, rather than as a vehicle of convenience for those invoking them. I think that in order to show that human rights are more than just competing claims, and that they reflect a sense that human beings have special worth we should turn to the increasingly influential idea that human rights are really about protecting human dignity (see Box 4).

Dignity

Modern rights theorists have sought to justify the existence and importance of rights by reference to some overriding value, such as freedom, fairness, autonomy, equality, personhood, or dignity. Following the German philosopher Immanuel Kant, some have sought to derive the logic of human rights from absolute moral principles which can be generated from the following imperatives: first, that each of us has to act according to the principles that we wish other rational beings to act on; and second, that a person should never be treated as a means to an end, but rather as an end in themselves. In the words of the modern philosopher Alan

Box 4 Frédéric Mégret et al *Human Dignity: A Special Focus on Vulnerable Groups*

The idea of dignity, then, might be something like: do not make me part of a process that is not really about me, do not make me a collateral victim of some larger goal. It is an appeal, in other words, to not submit individuals to social arrangements, but organize social arrangements according to individuals' dignity. The dignity approach is perhaps, in this respect, more satisfying than delineating a number of 'core rights', something which inevitably involves awkward and simplistic choices, in that among other things different rights matter differently to different people in different times.

All rights matter equally, and it is rather each right that has a core and a penumbra, where the core is precisely that area in which dignity is at stake.

Gerwith: 'agents and institutions are absolutely prohibited from degrading persons, treating them as if they had no rights or dignity'. This is often the starting point for rights theories that emphasize the importance of individual autonomy and agency as primordial values to be protected.

The modern philosopher Jürgen Habermas stresses the way in which human dignity is the route to egalitarian and universalistic laws and how human rights are bound up with the creation of democratic institutions that allow for a free flow of ideas and participation. For him 'The idea of human dignity is the conceptual hinge which connects the morality of equal respect for everyone with positive law and democratic lawmaking in such a way that their interplay could give rise to a political order founded on human rights, given suitable historical conditions.' In turn human rights 'anchor the ideal of a just society in the institutions of constitutional states themselves.'

Such philosophical excursions are helpful because they tell us *why* we might want to protect human rights. We can see that rights can be instrumental to building a society that allows people the freedom to develop as autonomous individuals, while allowing participation based on equality in the community's decision-making process. In other words, we can start to admit that political arrangements are useful for protecting human rights, not because every community must be about protecting God-given rights, or even respecting duties demanded by God or 'natural reason', but rather because human rights seem to prove a useful way to protect other values, such as dignity.

Of course one could ask at this point whether the concept of dignity deserves protection any more than human rights, and what, if anything, does the protection of dignity entail? While we can find all sorts of claims being premised on appeals to dignity, often on opposing sides of the argument, we might also suggest that contemporary concern for dignity, as evidenced by judicial reasoning, can be seen in at least four guises. First, the prohibition of all types of inhuman treatment, humiliation or degradation by one person over another; second, the assurance of the possibility for individual choice and the conditions for each individual's self-fulfilment, autonomy, or self-realization; third, the recognition that the protection of group identity and culture may be essential for the protection of personal dignity; and fourth, the creation of the necessary conditions for each individual to have their essential needs satisfied.

Christopher McCrudden has traced the increasing judicial popularity of dignity as the grounds for decision making in human rights cases not only under cases decided at the international level by the European and American Courts of Human Rights, but also from jurisdictions such as South Africa, Hungary, India, Israel, Germany, Canada, France, the United States, and the United Kingdom. His study shows that, even if we are still waiting for the term dignity to be given substantive meaning, the term provides 'a language in which judges can appear to justify how they deal with issues such as the weight of rights'.

Dignity is perhaps an explanatory term that helps us to see why some causes are preferred over others, it does not necessarily on its own justify a particular result. Freedom of expression is a matter of human dignity, but so are the restrictions designed to protect the private lives of others, to prevent hate speech, or to eliminate child pornography. Both sides of the debates over abortion or assisted suicide will appeal to human dignity as the guiding principle to determine who is right. As we will see when we consider the balancing of rights in Chapters 6 and 8, reasonable people can disagree about whose dignity should be prioritized. But looking at it this way, we can see that human rights cases are about more than interpreting the intention of the law-makers; they often involve choices about what sort of society we want.

Recent examples of judges justifying their human rights finding, by explaining that the result stems from the need to uphold the dignity of human beings, are to be found in decisions relating to life imprisonment. In Germany (and later at the European Court of Human Rights) it was found that life imprisonment without review could be incompatible with human rights as rehabilitation was required in 'any community that established human dignity as its centrepiece.'

The turn away from theory

Some philosophers have suggested that we abandon the quest for a convincing moral theory of why we have human rights. For Richard Rorty, it is a fact that: 'the emergence of the human rights culture seems to owe nothing to increased moral knowledge, and everything to hearing sad and sentimental stories', and that we should put foundationalist moral theories concerned with human rights behind us so that we can better 'concentrate our energies on

> ## Box 5 Michael Goodhart 'Human Rights and the Politics of Contestation'
>
> Human rights claims are political demands in the broadest sense. They are normative claims—claims about how things *should be*—but that is not the same as saying that they are claims about moral truth. They reflect the conviction that all people should be treated as moral equals entitled to certain essential freedoms. To invoke human rights is to challenge the order of things, to confront structures of power and privilege, 'natural' or arbitrary hierarchy, with the unshakable belief in freedom and equality for all. In this way, human rights are partisan or ideological. They take a particular side and reflect a particular perspective—that of the weak, the abused, the marginalized, the downtrodden.

manipulating sentiments, on sentimental education'. Others stress that human rights are claims about how the world should change and such claims are really about how things should be (see Box 5).

Lively discussion continues about the utility of human rights for progressive change. Many concerned with social justice question whether adopting a rights strategy might not result in entrenching existing property interests. Feminists continue to highlight the failure of human rights to address structural inequality between the sexes, issues of private violence against women, and the need for greater inclusion of women in decision making. Even reorienting human rights to address these issues could be considered simply a measure to reinforce stereotypes of women as victims of violence and in need of protection. At another level, as references to human rights feature increasingly in the discourse of Western leaders, some fear that human rights are becoming instrumentalized, deployed as excuses for intervention by powerful countries in the political, economic, and cultural life of weaker countries from the South. Lastly critics such as David Kennedy warn that the use of 'human rights vocabulary may have fully unintended negative consequences for other emanicipatory projects, including those relying on more religious, national or local energies.' Such criticism does not seek to deny that human rights exist. Indeed, human rights are sometimes under attack today, not because of doubts about their existence, but rather due to their omnipresence.

Kundera on human rights

The language of international human rights has become associated with all sorts of claims and disputes. Almost everyone now emphasizes their point of view in terms of an assertion or denial of rights. Indeed, for some in the West, it seems we have already entered an era when rights talk is becoming banal. Let us illustrate this with an excerpt from Milan Kundera's story 'The gesture of protest against a violation of human rights'. The story centres on Brigitte, who, following an argument with her German teacher (over the absence of logic in German grammar), drives through Paris to buy a bottle of wine from Fauchon.

> She wanted to park but found it impossible: rows of cars parked bumper to bumper lined the pavements for a radius of half a mile; after circling round and round for fifteen minutes, she was overcome with indignant astonishment at the total lack of space; she drove the car onto the pavement, got out and set out for the store.

As she approached the store she noticed something strange. Fauchon is a very expensive store, but on this occasion it was overrun by about 100 unemployed people all 'poorly dressed'. In Kundera's words:

> It was a strange protest: the unemployed did not come to break anything or to threaten anyone or to shout slogans; they just

wanted to embarrass the rich, and by their mere presence to spoil their appetite for wine and caviar.

Brigitte succeeded in getting her bottle of wine and returned to her car to find two policemen asking her to pay a parking fine. Brigitte started to abuse the policemen and when they pointed to the fact that the car was illegally parked and blocking the pavement, Brigitte pointed to all the rows of cars parked one behind the other:

'Can you tell me where I was supposed to park? If people are permitted to buy cars, they should also be guaranteed a place to put them, right? You must be logical!' she shouted at them.

Kundera tells the story to focus on the following detail:

at the moment when she was shouting at the policemen, Brigitte recalled the unemployed demonstrators in Fauchon's and felt a strong sense of sympathy for them: she felt united with them in a common fight. That gave her courage and she raised her voice; the policeman (hesitant, just like the women in fur coats under the gaze of the unemployed) kept repeating in an unconvincing and foolish manner words such as forbidden, prohibited, discipline, order, and in the end let her off without a fine.

Kundera tells us that during the dispute Brigitte kept rapidly shaking her head from left to right and at the same time lifting her shoulders and eyebrows. She again shakes her head from left to right when she tells the story to her father. Kundera writes:

We have encountered this movement before: it expresses indignant astonishment at the fact that someone wants to deny us our most self-evident rights. Let us therefore call this the gesture of protest against a violation of human rights.

For Kundera, it is the contradiction between the French revolutionary proclamations of rights and the existence of concentration camps in Russia that triggered the relatively recent Western enthusiasm for human rights:

> The concept of human rights goes back some two hundred years, but it reached its greatest glory in the second half of the 1970s. Alexander Solzhenitsyn had just been exiled from his country and his striking figure, adorned with beard and handcuffs, hypnotized Western intellectuals sick with a longing for the great destiny which had been denied them. It was only thanks to him that they started to believe, after a fifty-year delay, that in communist Russia there were concentration camps; even progressive people were now ready to admit that imprisoning someone for his opinions was not just. And they found an excellent justification for their new attitude: Russian communists violated human rights, in spite of the fact that these rights had been gloriously proclaimed by the French Revolution itself!

> And so, thanks to Solzhenitsyn, human rights once again found their place in the vocabulary of our times. I don't know a single politician who doesn't mention 10 times a day 'the fight for human rights' or 'violations of human rights'. But because people in the West are not threatened by concentration camps and are free to say and write what they want, the more the fight for human rights gains in popularity the more it loses any concrete content, becoming a kind of universal stance of everyone towards everything, a kind of energy that turns all human desires into rights. The world has become man's right and everything in it has become a right: the desire for love the right to love, the desire for rest the right to rest, the desire for friendship the right to friendship, the desire to exceed the speed limit the right to exceed the speed limit, the desire for happiness the right to happiness, the desire to publish a book the right to publish a book, the desire to shout in the street in the middle of the night the right to shout in the street. The unemployed have the right to occupy an expensive food store, the women in fur coats have the right to buy caviar, Brigitte has the right to park on the pavement and everybody, the unemployed, the women in fur coats as well as Brigitte, belongs to the same army of fighters for human rights.

Kundera's essay makes a few points about the changing world of human rights. First, for some people today, human rights are obvious, self-evident, and simply logical. There is often no challenge regarding the source of these rights or even the theoretical foundations of a rights claim. The foundations of the rights regime seem to us so solid that the act of invoking rights in itself seems to make you right.

Second, human rights are claims that automatically occur to one once one feels hard done by. A sense of injustice can breed a feeling that one has been denied one's rights. Appeals to rights as derived through irrefutable logic and entitlement are today somehow more immediately convincing than concepts such as 'social contract', 'the law of nature', or 'right reason'. Brigitte convinces the police through an appeal to a logical entitlement to a *right* to park on the pavement. An appeal for generosity, forgiveness, humanity, or charity would have involved a different gesture.

Third, a shared sense of grievance provides powerful succour for those claiming their 'rights'. When those of us who feel aggrieved stand together in protest we find strength through solidarity. The law itself may be the target of the protest. Outrage at law can somehow delegitimize such laws even in the eyes of law enforcers. Obedience to the law is a habit often related to the law's reasonableness. Invoking our human rights has become a way to challenge laws that we feel are unjust (even when the law has been adopted according to the correct procedures). In fact, human rights law has now developed so that, in almost all states, national law can be challenged for its lack of conformity with human rights. As laws are repealed and struck down, there is a valid perception that the legitimacy, or even legality, of all law has to be judged against human rights law. The hierarchy between human (or constitutional) rights law and normal national law is now mirrored at the international level in the hierarchy between general international law and certain 'superior' international law prohibitions (known as 'peremptory' or *'jus cogens'* norms).

Human rights operate from a higher plane and are used to criticize normal laws.

Fourth, appealing to rights and ensuring respect for rights is a way of, not only achieving a fixed goal, but changing the system we live in. Human rights are important as instruments for change in the world. Human rights have moved on from the idea of citizens' individual entitlements in a national revolutionary proclamation (such as the French Declaration of 1789 or the political settlements contained in the *Magna Carta* of 1215). Today, not only are human rights claims instrumental in changing national law, but human rights principles are considered relevant for international development assistance projects, facilitating transitional justice during regime change, dealing with post-conflict reconstruction, as well as tackling poverty and the effects of climate change.

Fifth, for some there is an historical association between human rights and Western preoccupations, and it has therefore been tempting to dismiss those who raise the issue of human rights as divorced from the actual deprivations they are talking about. The example of a rich girl complaining about lack of parking space is of course deliberately absurd and ironic. But Kundera's story illustrates how human rights outrage can quickly be made to seem ridiculous, even hypocritical, as certain Western governments selectively sanction and support human rights violations. It would, however, be a mistake to overemphasize the association of human rights with Western hypocrisy. In fact, the modern human rights movement and the complex normative international framework have grown out of a number of transnational and widespread movements. Human rights were and are increasingly invoked and claimed in the contexts of anti-imperialism, anti-apartheid, anti-racism, anti-Semitism, anti-homophobia, anti-islamophobia, and feminist and indigenous struggles everywhere. Western governments may recently have dominated the discourse at the highest international levels, but the chanting on the ground did not necessarily take its cue from them, nor did it sing to the West's tune.

Sixth, the sense of solidarity amongst those who believe they are the victims of a human rights violation can transcend class, gender, and other distinctions. This sense of connectedness is critical to understanding the changing world of human rights. The human rights movement involves Western-based mega organizations and tiny local fact-finding and advocacy groups toiling to reveal some of the worst abuses. Moroever, part of the justification for the primacy of certain human rights norms in public international law is that certain acts so offend the conscience of humanity that they should be prosecuted as crimes against humanity. It is the sense of common humanity and shared suffering that keeps the world of human rights moving and explains the *gesture of protest against a violation of human rights*.

Lastly, through the eyes of Kundera and Brigitte we observe several different logics of human rights depending on culture, time, place, and knowledge. This is a European story, set in the capital, and capturing the mood just at the end of the Cold War. There are contemporary African, Asian, or American stories which would be very different. But we suggest that Kundera helps us here because he identifies this special contemporary gesture as an internal human feeling which drives the discourse. The vocabulary of human rights is not a simple revelation of a deep universal structure which we all innately understand. Nor is it a language to be learned as an adult. It is the story of struggles concerning injustice, inhumanity, and better government. And at the same time, states may invoke human rights to further their own foreign policy goals. Unless we understand some of the driving forces behind human rights we risk missing the currents which will determine its future direction. Kundera's scepticism may jar—but it also strikes a chord. The contradiction between our commitment to the 'obvious' moral logic of human rights, and our cynicism towards certain rights claims has to be addressed head-on if we want to understand the world of human rights today.

For a contemporary heartfelt appeal to human rights we need look no further than a recent complaint concerning detention in Guantánamo Bay (see Box 6).

(see Box 6)

> **Box 6 Extract from a complaint submitted by Reprieve concerning a contract between the security company G4S and the US authorities responsible for detention in Guantánamo Bay**
>
> Emad Hassan is a Yemeni national who was seized while studying in Pakistan. During interrogation he was asked if he knew Al Qaeda, and replied yes. He was however referring to a small village named Al Qa'idah near his home in Yemen and not to the global terrorist network. This gross misunderstanding has formed the basis of Mr Hassan's detention without charge or trial at Guantánamo Bay for nearly twelve years.
>
> Mr Hassan travelled from Yemen to Pakistan to study poetry, but his studies ended when Pakistani forces detained him in a raid on his student housing. Mr Hassan was sold to American forces for a $5000 bounty and taken to Guantánamo Bay. In 2009, Mr Hassan was cleared for release by an inter-agency task force comprised of six different bodies of the U.S. government, including the FBI and CIA. Despite being cleared for release, Mr Hassan remains in indefinite detention.
>
> Mr Hassan has undertaken the longest hunger strike in Guantánamo. For the last seven years he has refused to eat, and has had to endure brutal force-feeding twice a day. Mr Hassan has been abusively force-fed more than five thousand times since 2007 as part of the military's efforts to break his spirit. He suffers from serious internal injuries as a result.

Box 6 Continued

Due to the force-feeding, Mr Hassan contracted severe pancreatitis and one of his nasal passages has completely closed up.

Mr Hassan has said, 'Sometimes I sit in the chair and vomit. Nobody says anything. Even if they turned their backs I would understand. I'm looking for humans. All I ask for is basic human rights.'

Chapter 2
Historical development and contemporary concerns

When officials or activists nowadays refer to 'human rights' they are almost certainly referring to the human rights recognized in international and national law, rather than rights in a moral or philosophical sense. Of course, philosophical debate will continue to illuminate (or sometimes obscure) the reasons *why* we think human rights are important and *how* to best develop them. But for the moment, the *content* of human rights (outside the philosophical realm) is usually understood by reference to the legal catalogue of human rights we find developed through international texts. This legal approach responds to demands for the concrete protection of what are perceived to be inherent natural rights, and goes some way to meeting the criticism that we are simply talking about anarchic desires. The shift to positive law also fixes these rights in an agreed written form. Hersch Lauterpacht's important book, *An International Bill of the Rights of Man*, published in 1945, drew on a range of natural rights thinking and constitutionally protected rights to argue for a written Bill of Rights to be protected through the UN.

A key text for us today is the Universal Declaration of Human Rights, adopted by the UN General Assembly in 1948 (see Annex). But the enumeration of human rights was not simply frozen by proclamation in 1948. Since that time dozens of treaties (agreements that create binding legal obligations for states) and intergovernmental Declarations have supplemented this proclamation of rights. In 1984, at the height of this flurry of writing up rights, Philip Alston suggested that new international human rights be subjected, like wine, to a 'quality control' by the UN General Assembly. The relevant UN resolution, adopted in 1986, suggested that international human rights instruments should:

(a) Be consistent with the existing body of international human rights law;
(b) Be of fundamental character and derive from the inherent dignity and worth of the human person;
(c) Be sufficiently precise to give rise to identifiable and practicable rights and obligations;
(d) Provide where appropriate, realistic and effective implementation machinery, including reporting systems;
(e) Attract broad international support.

Some may feel that various texts have failed this test, but, overall, the UN's core human rights instruments satisfy these criteria. Let us look in more detail at how this human rights catalogue came about.

Pre-Second World War

The historical development of the international protection of human rights deserves our attention as it tells us a lot about how and why states use human rights in international relations. The human rights story in the 20th century has multiple layers. At one level, human rights were invoked as a rationale for fighting the world wars. In 1915, in the context of the First World War, Sir Francis Younghusband set up an organization called the Fight for Right movement; one of its declared aims was 'To impress upon the country that we are fighting for something more than our own defence, that we are fighting the battle of all Humanity and to preserve Human Rights for generations to come.' At another, rather more academic, level the Chilean legal scholar Alejandro Alvarez, the Secretary General of the American Institute of International Law, was promoting in 1917 consideration of international recognition of rights for individuals and associations.

In his 1918 address to Congress, President Wilson spoke of his desire 'to create a world dedicated to justice and fair dealing'. His ideas were expanded in a proposed 'Fourteen Points' programme, which included explicit reference to rights to self-determination and statehood for nationalities seeking autonomy. Wilson's Fourteen Points formed the background to the negotiations to end the War even though they are not really reflected in the Versailles Peace Treaty in 1919, which included the Covenant of the League of Nations and the establishment of the International Labour Organization. The League was supposed to preserve international peace and security through the collective action of its member states against any state that resorted to war or the threat of war. Three developments are relevant: the minorities treaties, the development of international workers' rights, and the work on the abolition of slavery.

The Allied Powers and various Eastern European countries entered into a series of minority treaties and declarations for the protection of certain minority rights in Albania, Austria, Bulgaria, Czechoslovakia, Estonia, Finland, Greece, Hungary, Latvia, Lithuania, Poland, Romania, Turkey, and Yugoslavia. It was felt that with the redrawing of borders and the creation of new states, one should guard against the mistreatment of minorities in order to avoid disturbing the new 'peace of the world'. These treaties signalled the first multilateral efforts to protect the rights of specific groups of people at the international level. The treaties all contained similar provisions guaranteeing the protection of minority rights in the states party to the treaty, including the right to life and liberty for all inhabitants, and civil and political rights for nationals.

These League of Nations efforts to legally recognize and protect minority rights were an important development, as, on the one hand, they signalled attempts to protect individual rights through international law, and, on the other hand, they suggested that the way a state treats its inhabitants was now a matter of legitimate international concern. Yet, despite its important contribution to the protection of minority rights, the human rights protection offered under the League system was obviously limited to certain groups and certain countries.

The League of Nations was also active in the protection of workers' rights. The goal of 'fair and humane conditions of labour for men, women and children' was stated explicitly in the League Covenant. This goal became central to the work of the International Labour Organization (ILO), which continues today as one of the UN's specialized agencies. While the minorities treaties and the development of workers' rights can be seen as embryonic stages of the development of international human rights, we should be aware that these arrangements were put in place by governments *in their states' interests*. Individual rights were granted legal protection due to an individual's ties to a state; the conceit being that the state itself had been injured. States agreed to this arrangement as they considered such a move could reduce political tensions between states and so avoid war. Workers' rights were to be recognized and protected, because this was seen by some states as the best way to prevent their populations from turning to Communism thereby reducing the risk of revolution.

At the Paris Peace Conference in 1919 various delegates made proposals for the inclusion of respect for equality rights in the Covenant of the League of Nations. There was concern both for religious freedom and to ensure non-discrimination on the basis of race or nationality. The British delegate, Lord Cecil, even proposed that states have a right of 'intervention' against other states if these states engaged in forms of religious intolerance that would jeopardize global peace. The delegate of Japan, Baron

Makino, the Foreign Minister, specifically proposed the inclusion of a sentence that would have bound the member states to agree as soon as possible to accord equal and just treatment to alien nationals of League member states without distinction based on nationality or race.

Neither of these last two proposals was adopted. With regard to the failure to include a non-discrimination provision in the League Covenant, the late Antonio Cassese concluded:

> the Western great powers neither would nor could accept a principle that would have encroached heavily on their discriminatory practices against citizens of other areas of the world, and would have ended up threatening even the similar practices they still tolerated within their own systems (I have in mind above all, of course, racial discrimination in the United States).

We should also mention here the fight to outlaw the slave trade and to abolish slavery. Efforts to combat slavery had been ongoing in the 19th century. Although strategic and economic forces played a role in the abolition of slavery, there was also a genuine sentiment that slavery was inhuman; from the 1820s non-governmental organizations lobbied for international action to abolish slavery and the fight against slavery is sometimes seen as the beginning of the human rights movement, Anti-Slavery International considers itself the oldest international human rights organization in the world).

The League of Nations set up Commissions on slavery, adopted the 1926 Slavery Convention (supplemented in 1956), and developed conventions on the traffic in women and children to suppress what had been called in a 1910 Convention the 'White Slave Traffic'.

We should pause here to note briefly that today we are sadly faced with what are often called 'contemporary forms of slavery'. This includes trafficking in persons and forced labour. It is estimated by the ILO to cover over twenty million people, with illegal profits from forced labour amounting to US$150.2 billion per year (see Box 7). Contemporary forms of slavery at the centre of the UN's concerns include bonded labour, domestic servitude, early and forced marriage, child slave work, servile marriages, and caste-based forms of slavery. While trafficking includes not only persons trafficked for the sex trade, but also trafficking in persons for the removal of organs (see Box 8). Human rights thinking now seeks to consider the causes of such phenomena (see Box 9) to ensure that action moves beyond international cooperation, providing protection for the victims of trafficking. This is even harder when governments have tended to use the opportunity to clamp down on migrants, rather than pursue the traffickers and protect the trafficked.

With the League of Nations then we had strategic concern for certain national minorities, attention to the plight of workers, and paternalistic worries about women engaged in prostitution. We did not yet have meaningful international rights or obligations which protect human beings as human beings.

Box 7 ILO: 'Profits and Poverty'

In the 2012 survey, the ILO estimated that 20.9 million people are in forced labour globally, trafficked for labour and sexual exploitation or held in slavery-like conditions. The vast majority of the 20.9 million forced labourers—18.7 million (90 per cent)—are exploited in the private economy, by individuals or enterprises. Of these, 4.5 million (22 per cent) are victims of forced sexual exploitation, and 14.2 million (68 per cent) are victims of forced labour exploitation, primarily in agriculture, construction, domestic work, manufacturing, mining, and utilities. The remaining 2.2 million (10 per cent) are in state-imposed forms of forced labour, such as prisons, or in work imposed by military or paramilitary forces.

Box 8 UN Special Rapporteur Joy Ngozi Ezeilo: Report

In April 2013, five Kosovars, including three medical practitioners, were convicted of involvement in an organ trafficking syndicate that lured poor people from the Republic of Moldova, the Russian Federation, and Turkey to Kosovo to sell their kidneys and other organs to wealthy transplant recipients from Canada, Germany, Israel, and the United States of America. Recipients were charged up to $130,000. Victims, including five children, were promised payments of up to $26,000 and signed false documents in which they indicated that they were engaging in an altruistic donation to a relative. Many received no compensation or inadequate medical care.

Box 9 UN Special Rapporteur Urmila Bhoola: Report

While the profit motive drives the demand for forced labour and other contemporary forms of slavery, it is underpinned by 'push' factors such as increasing household vulnerability to income shocks, which push more households below the absolute poverty line; lack of education and illiteracy; as well as loss of work and deprivation of land, which force increased informal-sector work, migration and trafficking. The disproportionate impact of those factors on women and girls, who constitute more than half of the victims of forced labour, has been widely documented.

In the inter-war period there was some interest in developing the scope of international law to cover concern for individual rights. Albert de Lapradelle, a professor of international law at the University of Paris, presented the *Institut de droit international* (the Institute of International Law) with a draft 'Declaration of the International Rights of Man'. Influenced by the League of Nations minorities treaties, de Lapradelle sought to create a text that would be universal in nature whilst appealing to all states in the international community. André Mandelstam, a professor from Russia, developed a text that formed the basis of the eventual Declaration. Importantly, the final Declaration, approved in 1929 at a meeting of the distinguished members of the Institute in New York, did not refer to the rights of *citizens* but rather proclaimed rights to life, liberty, and property belonging to individual human beings. These rights had to be respected without any discrimination on grounds of nationality, sex, race, language, or religion. This text, however, remained the work of distinguished lawyers—powerful governments remained unenthusiastic about the international protection of human rights. In 1933, the delegate of Haiti, Antoine Frangulis, argued in vain at the League of Nations that states' obligations should go beyond the category of minorities and be extended through a general convention to offer the same protection and freedoms to everyone. Such a proposal, however, did not suit powerful states. The historian Paul Lauren quotes a British official, who said 'he did not wish to be quoted', as having said 'the acceptance of such a proposal by His Majesty's Government would be entirely impossible in view of our colonial experience'.

The Second World War

Almost from the beginning of the Second World War we find human rights being invoked. In 1939, the British author H. G. Wells wrote to *The Times* of London arguing for a discussion of the War Aims. He suggested the League of Nations was 'a poor and ineffective outcome of that revolutionary proposal to banish armed conflict from the world and inaugurate a new life for mankind'. Wells was 'terrified' of a repetition of the 'Geneva simulacrum'. In a follow-up letter, he appended a Declaration of Rights to define the spirit in which 'our people are more or less consciously fighting', as well as 'to appeal very forcibly to every responsive spirit under the yoke of the obscurantist and totalitarian tyrannies with which we are in conflict'. In other words, Wells considered these rights had universal appeal and gave sense to the fighting. This Declaration was developed into the *World Declaration of the Rights of Man*, and distributed to over 300 editors in forty-eight countries, generating worldwide interest. The ten paragraphs covered: discrimination; natural resources; health; education; paid employment; the right to buy and sell personal property; the right to move around the world freely; no imprisonment longer than six days without charge, and then no more than three months before a public trial; access to public records concerning individuals; and a prohibition on mutilation, sterilization, torture, and any bodily punishment.

The Declaration was included in Wells's widely distributed 1940 Penguin Special, entitled *The Rights of Man: Or What Are We Fighting For?* (see Figure 3). The book contained other declarations of rights, including a 1936 '*Complément à la Déclaration des Droits de l'homme*' prepared by the *Ligue des Droits de l'homme*.

Wells expressed the concern that laws were being passed that were disproportionate to the threats posed by traitors and foreigners (see Box 10). Interestingly, these concerns are remarkably relevant to present-day debates about terrorists, refugees, and others. The revised version of Wells's publication, the 1942 *Rights of the World Citizen*, ended with the following appeal:

> These are the rights of all human beings. They are yours whoever you are. Demand that your rulers and politicians sign and observe this declaration. If they refuse, if they quibble, they can have no place in the new free world that dawns upon mankind.

So the horrors of the Second World War provided a certain context for the development of the modern human rights movement. Wells discussed his Declaration with a variety of people, and most importantly with those who were being asked to fight. Their concern was not only to 'put down violence' but more significantly

A PENGUIN SPECIAL

What are we fighting for?

H. G. WELLS
ON
THE RIGHTS OF MAN

3. The H. G. Wells paperback; the Allies are said to have dropped the Declaration behind enemy lines. Wells's Declaration of Rights was widely distributed and translated into not only European languages but also into Chinese, Japanese, Arabic, Urdu, Hindi, Bengali, Gujerati, Hausa, Swahili, Yoruba, Zulu, and Esperanto.

Box 10 H. G. Wells, *The Rights of Man: Or What Are We Fighting For?*

... there has accumulated a vast tangle of emergency legislation, regulations, barriers and restraints, out of all proportion to and often missing and distorting the needs of the situation. For the restoration and modernisation of human civilisation, this exaggerated outlawing of the fellow citizen whom we see fit to suspect as a traitor or revolutionary and also of the stranger within our gates, has to be restrained and brought back within the scheme of human rights.

'they had been stirred profoundly by those outrages upon human dignity perpetrated by the Nazis'.

In 1941, in a related (but not necessarily connected) move, US President Franklin Roosevelt famously proclaimed, in his annual State of the Union address to Congress, four essential human freedoms: freedom of speech, freedom of worship, freedom from want, and freedom from fear. The speech also explained that: 'Freedom means the supremacy of human rights everywhere.' During the same year, President Roosevelt and Prime Minister Churchill issued a joint declaration known now as the 'Atlantic Charter', which set out their vision for the post-war world. The joint declaration stated that:

> after the final destruction of the Nazi tyranny, they hope to see established a peace which will afford to all nations the means of dwelling in safety within their own boundaries, and which will afford assurance that all the men in all the lands may live out their lives in freedom from fear and want.

In turn, representatives of twenty-six Allied nations later signed a Declaration by United Nations on 1 January 1942, subscribing to the purposes and principles in the Atlantic Charter and stating that they were:

> convinced that complete victory over their enemies is essential to defend life, liberty, independence and religious freedom, and to preserve human rights and justice in their own lands as well as in other lands, and that they are now engaged in a common struggle against savage and brutal forces seeking to subjugate the world.

In addition to the Allied nations at war with the Axis powers, a further twenty-one states had also signed the Declaration by August 1945. This combined group would become the core of the fifty-one original member states of the United Nations Organization. The UN Charter adopted in 1945 commits the Organization to encouraging respect for human rights and obligates the member states to cooperate with the UN for the promotion of universal respect for, and observance of, human rights. However, efforts to include a legally binding bill of rights at that time came to nothing. Instead, the immediate focus was on the prosecution of international crimes.

Prosecution of international crimes

At the end of the Second World War, the victorious powers established the Nuremberg International Military Tribunal to try the 'major war criminals of the European Axis', and the Tokyo Tribunal to try the 'major war criminals in the Far East'. These two Tribunals tried individuals for crimes against peace (aggression), war crimes, and crimes against humanity (in connection with aggression or war crimes). The Nuremberg Tribunal sentenced twelve defendants to death, and five defendants to long sentences of imprisonment. The Tokyo Tribunal sentenced seven defendants to death and sixteen received life sentences. For some, the purpose of these trials was to demonstrate that the Allies were better than the Fascists, and to serve an educational purpose. However, the trials can also be seen in other ways. From one perspective, they represented victor's justice: war crimes which may have been committed by the Allies were not tried, and the charges of crimes against peace and crimes against humanity seemed to rest on rather uncertain legal ground.

From another perspective, the Nuremberg judgment initiated a new way of thinking about international law and its impact on the individual. The defendants were seen as having violated the international law of war, a law that could be gleaned from general principles of justice applied by military courts. The Tribunal declared: 'This law is not static, but by continual adaptation follows the needs of a changing world.' The Tribunal went on to dismiss any notion that this law was confined to duties for states or that individuals could hide behind traditional notions of state immunity: 'Crimes against international law are committed by men, not by abstract entities, and only by punishing individuals who commit such crimes can the provisions of international law be enforced.' Furthermore, the development of the category of crimes referred to as 'crimes against humanity' finally cemented the idea that international obligations are owed to individuals because of their human worth, rather than because they are protected abroad by their state of nationality, or are protected through a particular treaty protecting national minorities.

The phrase 'crimes against humanity' is sometimes traced back to 1890 when it was used by George Washington Williams, an African American religious minister and member of the Ohio state legislature, in a letter of protest about the State of the Congo under the Belgian King Leopold II (see Figure 4). He wrote to the US Secretary State that 'The State of Congo is in no sense deserving your confidence or support. It is actively engaged in the slave trade and is guilty of many crimes against humanity.'

Later on we find a 1915 Joint Declaration by France, Great Britain, and Russia concerning the Armenians. The diplomatic exchanges show that the original Russian draft declaration referred to crimes

4. George Washington Williams, the American pastor, attorney, and historian who exposed King Leopold's regime in the Congo in his Open Letter in 1890.

'against Christianity and civilization'. The French were, however, worried that care should be taken that the Muslim population living under French and British rule would not conclude that the interests of these two powers only led to action when Christians were threatened. The British concurred that the phrase could be omitted. The Armenian *Dachnaksoutiun* appealed to the Imperial Russian Foreign Ministry to hold the members of the government individually responsible 'for the love of humanity'. Rather than omitting the reference to Christianity, the Russians successfully proposed to replace 'Christianity' with 'humanity'. The final Declaration referred to specific sites and stated that in view 'of those new crimes of Turkey against humanity and civilization', the Allied governments were to 'hold personally responsible' all those 'implicated in such massacres'. In fact, the promise by Turkey in 1920 to hand over those persons whom the Allies considered responsible for the massacres was contained in a treaty that never entered into force, and the later 1923 peace treaty included a declaration of amnesty.

The category of crimes against humanity was used in the 1945 Nuremberg Charter to ensure that the deportation of *Germans* by Germans to the concentration camps, and their subsequent mistreatment and extermination, could be prosecuted. Under the international laws of war at that time, the way in which a government treated its own nationals (no matter how heinous) was considered by international law as exclusively a matter of domestic jurisdiction, rather than an issue of international concern. The concept of crimes against humanity was therefore used to include these atrocities as part of the international prosecution. The Allies were, however, careful to ensure that crimes against humanity were included only to the extent they were connected to the war. At the time, this was to ensure the concept could not be easily extended to prosecute those who might be accused of mistreating the inhabitants of the colonies or the United States. Even if crimes against humanity might be seen by some to be something different from human rights, today such crimes (together with genocide and ethnic cleaning) preoccupy a number of human rights organizations and command attention. There is no longer any need to show a connection between the alleged offences and an armed conflict.

Raphael Lemkin, a determined Jewish lawyer from Poland, became obsessed with preventing massacres after learning of the fate of the Armenians in 1915 and the Assyrians in 1933. At a Conference on the unification of criminal law in Madrid he proposed a catalogue of new offences against the law of nations: crimes of barbarity; crimes of vandalism; and provoking a catastrophe by disrupting international communication or through contamination. Lemkin was seeking to link a concern about individual rights with anxiety over phenomena that threatened the international community. He sought to create crimes which could and would be universally suppressed (see Box 11).

Frustrated by his inability to gain any support for action on the crime of barbarity, Lemkin decided to coin a new word to encapsulate his concerns and garner attention. An accomplished linguist (he apparently mastered fourteen languages) he came up with the word 'genocide' (*genos* from the Greek for a tribe or race, *cedere* being the Latin verb to kill). When he failed to have his crime recognized in the judgment of the Nuremberg Tribunal he set about convincing states at the United Nations to adopt a new international text on genocide.

The General Assembly adopted the *Convention on the Prevention and Punishment of the Crime of Genocide* on 9 December 1948. The Convention declares that genocide is a crime under international law whether committed in time of peace or of war. It defines genocide as any of the following acts committed with intent to destroy, in whole or in part, a national, ethnical, racial, or religious group, as such: killing members of the group; causing serious bodily or mental harm to members of the group; deliberately inflicting on the group conditions of life calculated to bring about

> **Box 11 Raphael Lemkin: report presented in Madrid 1933**
>
> The author proposes the introduction of two new crimes, namely barbarity and vandalism, into the penal codes of individual states, these crimes to be judged in that country, where the criminal is caught, regardless of his citizenship or of the country in which the crime was committed by him. Their text should be as follows:
>
> Article 1. Whosoever, out of hatred towards a racial, religious or social collectivity, or with a view to the extermination thereof, undertakes a punishable action against the life, bodily integrity, liberty, dignity or economic existence of a person, belonging to such a collectivity, is liable, for the crime of barbarity...The offender will be liable to the same penalty, if his action is directed against a person who has declared his solidarity with such a collectivity or has intervened in favour thereof.
>
> Article 2. Whosoever, either out of hatred towards a racial religious or social collectivity, or with a view to the extermination thereof, destroys its cultural or artistic works, will be liable for the crime of vandalism...

its physical destruction in whole or in part; imposing measures intended to prevent births within the group; and forcibly transferring children of the group to another group.

Importantly, the Convention makes the individual perpetrator punishable 'whether they are constitutionally responsible rulers, public officials, or private individuals'. The Convention has been central to the work of the ad hoc international criminal tribunals established by the Security Council to deal with crimes committed in the former Yugoslavia and Rwanda.

The former Prime Minister of Rwanda, Jean Kambanda, was sentenced to life imprisonment for genocide and crimes against

5. Radislav Krstić: Commander of the Drina Corps, a formation of the Bosnian Serb Army, and, later, facing charges of genocide.

humanity. Radislav Krstić, Chief of Staff of the Bosnian Serb Army (Drina Corps) (see Figure 5), was sentenced to thirty-five years' imprisonment for aiding and abetting genocide in Srebrenica by allowing military personnel under his command to be used for the murder of about 8,000 men (see Box 12).

The International Criminal Court, which came into existence in 2002, now has jurisdiction over certain individuals not only for genocide and war crimes but also for a long list of crimes against humanity (see Box 13). It is possible that it will have jurisdiction over the crime of aggression from 2017.

In contrast to the Tribunals just mentioned, which were set up to address particular conflicts, and in the case of Nuremberg and Tokyo only to try the leadership of the defeated enemy, the International Criminal Court can try any individual who has the nationality of a state that has accepted to be bound by the Court's Statute, or who has committed this kind of international crime in such a state. There are now over 120 such states, including

Box 12 International Criminal Tribunal for the former Yugoslavia: *Krstić* case

By seeking to eliminate a part of the Bosnian Muslims, the Bosnian Serb forces committed genocide. They targeted for extinction the forty thousand Bosnian Muslims living in Srebrenica, a group which was emblematic of the Bosnian Muslims in general. They stripped all the male Muslim prisoners, military and civilian, elderly and young, of their personal belongings and identification, and deliberately and methodically killed them solely on the basis of their identity. The Bosnian Serb forces were aware, when they embarked on this genocidal venture, that the harm they caused would continue to plague the Bosnian Muslims. The Appeals Chamber states unequivocally that the law condemns, in appropriate terms, the deep and lasting injury inflicted, and calls the massacre at Srebrenica by its proper name: genocide. Those responsible will bear this stigma, and it will serve as a warning to those who may in future contemplate the commission of such a heinous act.

Afghanistan, Australia, Bangladesh, Burundi, Canada, Chile, Colombia, Democratic Republic of Congo, France, Germany, Italy, Japan, Jordan, Kenya, Liberia, Nigeria, Palestine, Peru, Senegal, Sierra Leone, Tunisia, Uganda, and the United Kingdom. Additionally, if the Security Council considers that a situation threatens international peace and security, it can refer that situation to the Court's Prosecutor for investigation and eventual prosecution. This happened in 2005 with regard to the situation in Dafur (Sudan) and in 2011 with regard to Libya.

The first conviction at the International Criminal Court was Thomas Lubango Dyilo (from the rebel Patriotic Force for the Liberation of Congo) who was sentenced in 2012 to fourteen years imprisonment for enlisting and conscripting of children under the age of 15, and using them to participate actively in hostilities

Box 13 Statute of the International Criminal Court, Article 7: crimes against humanity

1. For the purpose of this Statute, 'crime against humanity' means any of the following acts when committed as part of a widespread or systematic attack directed against any civilian population, with knowledge of the attack:

   (a) Murder;

   (b) Extermination;

   (c) Enslavement;

   (d) Deportation or forcible transfer of population;

   (e) Imprisonment or other severe deprivation of physical liberty in violation of fundamental rules of international law;

   (f) Torture;

   (g) Rape, sexual slavery, enforced prostitution, forced pregnancy, enforced sterilization, or any other form of sexual violence of comparable gravity;

   (h) Persecution against any identifiable group or collectivity on political, racial, national, ethnic, cultural, religious, gender... or other grounds that are universally recognized as impermissible under international law, in connection with any act referred to in this paragraph or any crime within the jurisdiction of the Court;

   (i) Enforced disappearance of persons;

   (j) The crime of apartheid;

   (k) Other inhumane acts of a similar character intentionally causing great suffering, or serious injury to body or to mental or physical health.

(see Figure 6). The second conviction was Germain Katanga who was sentenced to twelve years' imprisonment on one count of crime against humanity (murder) and four counts of war crimes (murder, attacking a civilian population, destruction of property, and pillaging) committed on 24 February 2003 during the attack

6. Child soldiers in the Democratic Republic of Congo.

on the village of Bogoro, in the Ituri district of the Democratic Republic of Congo.

At the time of writing, the Prosecutor is also investigating the situations in Uganda, Democratic Republic of Congo, Central

African Republic, Kenya, Libya, Côte d'Ivoire, and Mali. In addition, the Prosecutor is examining allegations of international crimes committed on the territories of Honduras, Ukraine, Iraq, and Palestine. The Prosecutor is assessing if there were genuine national proceedings carried out in Afghanistan, Georgia, Guinea, Colombia, and Nigeria.

The Court is not without its critics. Following the publicity given to the International Court's arrest warrants for the leaders of the rebel Lord's Resistance Army in Uganda, some argued that the existence of this Court disrupted the peace negotiations, generated a further round of violence, and exposed potential witnesses to unacceptable risks. A further line of criticism argues that the international tribunals shift the focus away from the communities that need to come to terms with their own history, and delay the development of national legal systems that can enjoy the confidence of the people. Lastly, critics also point to the focus on Africa and the slow rate of convictions. All these points deserve consideration, but the Court cannot ever be expected to round up the world's worst international criminals around the globe. The existence of the Court is plainly not enough to stem the tide of vicious human rights violations—realistically, only a handful of people will be tried in the coming years. Nevertheless, we must hope that some people in some places are dissuaded from committing human rights violations. Importantly, everyone has been put on notice that he or she could end up as a defendant before this international Court. Perhaps just as significantly, the prospects of prosecution before a national court at home or abroad have been considerably enhanced.

Lemkin's ideas may have been ahead of their time, but today the idea of framing threats as international crimes has taken on a dominant position among the professionals that are charged with human rights protection. International human rights inquiries and press releases are often framed as concerns about possible international crimes; all three UN High Commissioners for

Human Rights appointed from 2004 to 2014 have brought with them experience from the world of international criminal tribunals; major non-governmental organizations have programmes on international justice or international crimes; and in 2014 African states sought to add a Criminal Chamber to their new African Court of Justice and Human Rights. International criminal prosecution is increasingly seen as the obvious response to injustice. Gerry Simpson has even highlighted how those opposed to military intervention (and in particular the Iraq invasion of 2003) now see such action as raising questions of legality, criminality, and international prosecution. In the past critics might have simply branded such military adventures as 'mistakes'.

The Universal Declaration of Human Rights

Let us leave the contemporary prosecutions of international crimes and return to the end of the Second World War. The establishment of the United Nations signalled the beginning of a period of unprecedented international concern for the protection of human rights. Under the auspices of the UN, several key instruments were established for the promotion and protection of human rights. The day after the adoption of the Genocide Convention, the General Assembly proclaimed the Universal Declaration of Human Rights 'as a common standard of achievement for all peoples and all nations' (see the Annex to this book). Having given up on fixing the precise philosophical origins of human rights, the major controversy for diplomats at the time of the Declaration's eventual adoption grew out of the antagonism between the Communist bloc and the West. The Soviet Union's representatives stated that they wanted better implementation of economic and social rights; but were also concerned that the Declaration would be used to interfere with matters of national sovereignty. Other complaints from Communist states referred to the failure of the Declaration to ensure that Fascism could not exploit democratic institutions to return to power. The Communist bloc would have explicitly precluded freedom of expression for

Fascists. In her fascinating history of the drafting of the Declaration, Mary Anne Glendon highlights the Soviets' preoccupation concerning the inclusion of a right to leave one's country and the failure to frame the rights in terms of what was allowed under the law of the state.

An evaluation of the relevance of the Universal Declaration would have to conclude that the Declaration has had a huge influence, both in terms of spreading the philosophy of human rights, and in terms of inspiring legal texts and decisions. Translated into over 300 languages, it has often been at the heart of demands made by peoples and individuals around the world that their rights be respected and protected. Several constitutions have taken its provisions as the basis for a bill of rights, and national and international courts have invoked the Declaration in their judgments. The member states of the UN have come to acknowledge that their human rights obligations are now 'beyond question' (See Box 14).

Universality

Are human rights now really universal? While it is true that African and Asian governments currently accept the Universal

> **Box 14 World Summit Outcome adopted by Heads of State and Government, 2005**
>
> We reaffirm the solemn commitment of our States to fulfil their obligations to promote universal respect for and the observance and protection of all human rights and fundamental freedoms for all in accordance with the Charter, the Universal Declaration of Human Rights and other instruments relating to human rights and international law. The universal nature of these rights and freedoms is beyond question.

Declaration and have signed and ratified various human rights treaties, such a formalistic response fails to capture the cultural differences in the appreciation of what human rights are about, and what new obligations ought to be included in the catalogue. Scholars such as Abdullahi An-Naʿim suggest that the feeling of a lack of cultural legitimacy can be addressed through a cross-cultural critique of behaviour which builds on locally accepted norms. As he puts it 'I believe not only that universal cultural legitimacy is necessary, but also that it is possible to develop it retrospectively in relation to fundamental human rights through enlightened interpretations of cultural norms'. The pressing issue is how we can now build a universal appreciation for these ideas.

But even if one might work towards universal acceptance of the duty to respect others' dignity, governments remain divided on some basic issues. Some governments object to the demand that human rights include the concept of 'collective rights' or 'group rights' for peoples. This objection is based on a particular appreciation of what human rights should be about (for example, some derive human rights from the starting point that there is an imagined social contract between the *individual* and the state). It is also based on a fear that recognizing a people as having a collective human right will be a step towards a claim that such a people have the right to their own state. Similarly, contemporary debate about economic, social, and cultural rights is sometimes held hostage by those who consider that one cannot conceive of rights to housing, health, and education as judicially enforceable entitlements—for these people it is better to see such 'so called rights' as aspirations, public policy goals, or simply socialist rhetoric. But today these rights are in fact enshrined in treaties and subject to international supervision and complaints mechanism in the same way as civil and political rights. We will consider some examples in Chapter 7.

So, even if there is apparent universal acceptance by governments of the human rights message, there is still discord over what constitutes a human right and how rights should be implemented. Clearly a starting point should be enforcement at the national level. International human rights law is supposed to be translated into the national legal order so that the rights are effective with meaningful remedies for the victims of violations. Needless to say, this is by no means a perfect process and many rights get 'lost in translation'.

Furthermore, as we move from lofty proclamations to detailed implementation and accountability, we encounter the reaction that rights have to be implemented according to the cultural and economic context of the country concerned. This is sometimes seen as the death knell for the credibility of the so-called 'universality' of human rights. It is, however, a mistake to imagine that human rights can, or should, operate divorced from any local context. Even the application of an accepted right, such as the right to life, can lead to different interpretations depending on the country context. In a case concerning a dispute between two estranged parents of frozen embryos, the European Court of Human Rights held that:

> in the absence of any European consensus on the scientific and legal definition of the beginning of life, the issue of when the right to life begins comes within the margin of appreciation which the Court generally considers that States should enjoy in this sphere.

The international judges were divided over the separate question of whether the destruction of the embryos constituted a violation of the mother's right to respect for her private life. Again, they considered the matter was better left to national legislators than to a judicial divination of overriding human rights principles. In different countries, the father's withdrawal of consent to implantation of an embryo has been given a different weight. In the absence of 'international consensus' or 'common ground' among European states, the human rights Court found that the legislation before the Court (which required the father's consent before implantation of the embryo) was within the margin allowed to states and their legislatures by the European Convention on Human Rights. In short, human rights law does allow for different approaches to implementation across cultures and nations. At the same time, there is, of course, a sense that there is some core content to each right, and that failure to respect this content can be universally condemned. Clearly now the prohibitions on crimes against humanity and genocide apply in all places and at all times. Other rights related to torture, slavery, or forced labour contain core content that cannot be adjusted to take into account local conditions. However, when it comes, for example, to rights to freedom of expression, privacy, access to justice, food, water, health housing, and education, we shall see that the issues become more complex as we need to consider how to weigh competing interests.

The International Covenants

Following the adoption of the Universal Declaration, the UN's Human Rights Commission began work on a legally binding text in the form of a treaty together with measures for implementation. Governments had decided that there should be a binding multilateral treaty on human rights to complement the existing Declaration. Due to political disagreements about including all types of rights within one treaty, the General Assembly requested the Commission to draft two separate covenants—one on 'civil and political' rights, and another on 'economic, social and cultural' rights. On 16 December 1966, the General Assembly adopted the *International Covenant on Economic, Social and Cultural Rights* and the *International Covenant on Civil and Political Rights*. Both came into force for the relevant states in 1976.

The International Covenant on Economic, Social and Cultural Rights covers human rights in areas including education, food, housing, and health care, as well as the right to work and to just and favourable conditions of work. A state that becomes a party to the Covenant agrees to take steps for the progressive realization of Covenant rights to the full extent of that state's available resources. It was accepted from the outset that the scope of a state's obligations will depend on the circumstances.

The International Covenant on Civil and Political Rights safeguards rights such as rights to life, liberty, fair trial, freedom of movement, thought, conscience, peaceful assembly, family, and privacy. It also prohibits slavery; torture; cruel, inhuman or degrading treatment and punishment; discrimination; arbitrary arrest; and imprisonment for debt.

Both Covenants start with an Article that reads:

> All peoples have the right of self-determination. By virtue of that right they freely determine their political status and freely pursue their economic, social and cultural development.

These two Covenants, taken together with the Universal Declaration, are sometimes referred to as the 'International Bill of Rights'. Each Covenant has an Optional Protocol which allows for individuals to complain to the relevant UN monitoring Committee that a state is in violation of the Covenant. There are 115 states that have accepted this procedure for civil and political rights (the Protocol was adopted alongside the Covenant in 1966), and twenty for economic, social, and cultural rights (the Protocol only having been adopted in 2008).

The ideological and political struggle between the superpowers dominated the international human rights agenda during the 1950s, and the initial post-war momentum that led to the adoption of the Universal Declaration diminished considerably. However, the human rights impetus at the United Nations gained momentum again in the early 1960s, primarily as a result of decolonization. Most of the African and Asian countries that had been under colonial rule when the UN was founded were now becoming independent. Many of these states had a particular interest in human rights issues as a result of their colonial history. UN membership quickly doubled and, by the mid-1960s, developing countries became the largest voting bloc in the General Assembly. The participation of these states stimulated the human rights activities of the UN and took the international human rights agenda in new directions.

Other human rights treaties adopted at the United Nations

In addition to the so-called 'International Bill of Human Rights', the UN system is the source of a number of other international human rights instruments. Some of which we will briefly mention. The *International Convention on the Elimination of All Forms of Racial Discrimination* came into force in 1969 and prohibits:

> any distinction, exclusion, restriction or preference based on race, colour, descent, or national or ethnic origin which has the purpose or effect of nullifying or impairing the recognition, enjoyment or exercise, on an equal footing, of human rights and fundamental freedoms in the political, economic, social, cultural or any other field of public life.

The *Convention on the Elimination of All Forms of Discrimination against Women* is designed to ensure women have equal access to political and public life as well as education, health, and employment. Under this Convention, which entered into force in 1981, states are also obliged to take all appropriate measures:

> To modify the social and cultural patterns of conduct of men and women, with a view to achieving the elimination of prejudices and customary and all other practices which are based on the idea of the

inferiority or the superiority of either of the sexes or on stereotyped roles for men and women.

The *Convention against Torture and Other Cruel, Inhuman or Degrading Treatment or Punishment* came into force in 1987. The Convention includes a definition of torture (for the purposes of the Convention), and insists that any party to it undertakes obligations: to take measures to prevent acts of torture in any territory under its jurisdiction; not to return any person to a state where there are substantial grounds for believing that that person would be in danger of being subjected to torture; and to ensure that acts of torture can be prosecuted in the courts of that state even though those acts occurred abroad. We examine the prohibition on torture and other inhuman and degrading treatment in Chapter 4.

The *Convention on the Rights of the Child* defines a child as 'every human being below the age of eighteen unless under the law applicable to the child, majority is attained earlier'. It seeks to protect children from practices that particularly endanger their welfare, including economic exploitation, trafficking, illicit use of drugs, and all forms of sexual exploitation and abuse. The guiding principles of the Convention are the need to take into account the child's best interests, non-discrimination, and respect for the wishes of the child. The Convention entered into force in 1990 and has become the most widely ratified of all UN human rights treaties. The only UN member state not to have become a party to the Convention is the United States. In addition the Holy See (the Vatican), Niue, and the State of Palestine have all become parties to the Convention.

The *International Convention on the Protection of the Rights of All Migrant Workers and their Families* entered into force in 2003. Unfortunately, the states that have accepted obligations under this treaty are mostly states that *export* migrant workers rather than those that host them. This diminishes the effectiveness and scope of the treaty obligations, and means that those states that host migrant workers avoid the reach of this treaty and the prospect of supervision by the monitoring body.

Two new human rights treaties were adopted at the end of 2006. The first is the *International Convention on the Rights of Persons with Disabilities*. Key rights concern the right to make decisions, the right to marry, the right to have a family, the right to work, and the right to education. States are obliged to refrain from discrimination on grounds of disability and to take measures to eliminate such discrimination by 'any person, organization or private enterprise'. The second is the *International Convention for the Protection of All Persons from Enforced Disappearance*. It establishes the prospect of national prosecutions and extradition for the crime of enforced disappearance. This crime is defined as:

> the arrest, detention, abduction or any other form of deprivation of liberty committed by agents of the State or by persons or groups of persons acting with the authorization, support or acquiescence of the State, followed by a refusal to acknowledge the deprivation of liberty or by concealment of the fate or whereabouts of the disappeared person, which place such a person outside the protection of the law.

Even if there is a perennial mantra that the United Nations should focus less on 'standard setting' and more on 'implementation', claims for 'new rights' will not go away. In addition to the rights of indigenous peoples (now enshrined in the 2007 UN Declaration), there are ongoing discussions among states for the elaboration of a text on 'the rights and dignity of older persons'.

Scholars have started to analyse how new rights campaigns are formed, and what makes them successful. One collection of essays looks at recent campaigns that are presented as international human rights issues, and includes the following: children born of war time rape; Dalit rights; the rights of lesbians and gay men; HIV/AIDS; disability rights; female genital mutilation; extreme poverty; and the right to water. Understanding how an issue gets absorbed into the international human rights apparatus tells us a lot about the dynamics of human rights today. Clifford Bob explains the findings as follows:

> First, politicized groups frame long felt grievances as normative claims. Second, they place these rights on the international agenda by convincing gatekeepers in major rights organizations to accept them…Third, states and international bodies, often under pressure from gatekeepers and aggrieved groups accept new norms. Finally, national institutions implement the norms.

Protecting human rights through international and regional supervision

Human rights treaties and declarations, and a series of parallel developments at the regional levels: at the Organization of American States, the Council of Europe, the African Union, the Arab League, and the Association of South East Nations (ASEAN) articulate a vast range of rights and supposedly testify to governments' stated desire to protect human rights. But do such texts make a difference? Clearly the daily evidence of human rights violations suggests that drafting declarations and signing treaties is not enough. Considerable effort has, however, been expended to make these guarantees more effective. This has been undertaken on a number of fronts.

First, expert monitoring bodies have been established to examine the reports of governments on how they fulfil their human rights obligations. This involves a 'constructive dialogue' over two or three days and results in 'concluding observations' from the relevant committee. Some monitoring bodies also engage in fact-finding and country visits. In the context of the prevention of torture, the Council of Europe's expert body makes periodic and ad hoc visits to places of detention in forty-seven European states (over 365 visits so far), and the UN's committee undertakes similar visits to those states that have ratified the relevant treaty; so far they have visited places of detention in Mauritius, Maldives, Sweden, Benin, Mexico, Paraguay, Honduras, Cambodia, Lebanon, Bolivia, Liberia, Ukraine, Brazil, Mali, Argentina, Kyrgyzstan, New Zealand, Peru, Gabon, Nicaragua, and Azerbaijan.

Second, under most human rights treaties, complaints can be brought by aggrieved individuals against the state at the international level (usually only against those states that specifically recognize a 'right to complain' under the treaty or relevant Protocol). In addition to the Protocols to the two Covenants already mentioned, the Conventions on persons with disabilities, the rights of the child, and discrimination against women have recently been supplemented with similar Protocols allowing for such complaints. The other human rights treaties also include mechanisms that allow individuals to communicate individual complaints. This right to complain under the UN treaties is remarkably underutilized. In part this may be due to victims fearing reprisals, but in part it is because these possibilities are not well-known. The procedures have nevertheless been resorted to with some success by those fearing deportation or extradition to a country where there is a real risk of torture or the death penalty.

Here, a special mention needs to be made of the remarkable work of the regional bodies such as the European and Inter-American Courts of Human Rights and the European, Inter-American Commission and African Commissions on Human Rights. These bodies have developed an impressive case-law, which has not only led to a deeper understanding of the scope of human rights, but also to some very concrete protection and changes in the law. Although in most cases where the state loses, the decision merely involves a declaration that the state has violated human rights and must pay reparations, in some cases the Court will order that an individual must not be deported, or must be released from detention, or even that the law must change.

The African system has now established a Court of Human and Peoples' Rights, although relatively few African states presently allow for this Court to receive complaints by individuals or civil society organizations (Burkina Faso, Malawi, Mali, Tanzania, Ghana, Rwanda, Cote d'Ivoire). The Arab League has agreed to establish a new Arab Court of Human Rights, which again does not allow for complaints to be brought without a separate agreement from the state concerned. The new Declaration on Human Rights from the Association of South East Asian Nations (ASEAN) does not foresee a complaints procedure.

Third, consolidation of these rights in treaties can empower victims to remind the authorities of their international obligations, and this in turn legitimizes a whole series of demands and protests at the national level, whether through judicial or other processes.

Finally, in certain cases, such as genocide, torture, and enforced disappearances, the treaties establish the legal framework for the prosecution of individuals who are apprehended outside their own country. The torture treaty has also been used to overcome legal arguments that certain individuals enjoy international immunity from such prosecutions (this is what happened to Senator Pinochet when he was detained in London).

Relying on these treaties to improve human rights protection nevertheless remains unsatisfactory. The monitoring of governments' compliance with their treaty obligations largely depends on self-reporting and 'shadow reporting' by civil society. The monitoring bodies (comprised of independent experts) do an admirable job of analysing the human rights situation in a country, and in recommending the steps a government needs to take to bring itself into compliance with its human rights obligations. But, in the context of a state's stubborn refusal to cooperate, the monitoring bodies have only the power of publicity. Publicity is only effective to the extent that others report and care about the exposed shortcomings of the government in question.

It is hard to test the actual impact of these treaties. The translation of the principles is subtle and takes effect over time. We will never know all the human rights violations that were actually avoided due to officials thinking twice before taking action that would violate a human rights treaty. There is, however, concrete evidence of improvements having been made as a result of both recommendations contained in the reports of the UN monitoring bodies, and the decisions and judgments of the regional bodies and Courts. In some cases, national policies have been rethought to bring them into compliance with human rights principles, and in other cases, individual complaints have given rise to radical changes in law and practice.

While the Inter-American, European, and African systems may be the most well-established of the regional mechanisms, the existence of new texts agreed in the Arab and South East Asian (ASEAN) regions means that we may see healthy development of human rights thinking based on a sensibility to human rights that is more local, and less dependent on the idea that these texts are a European legacy from the trauma of the Second World War. The regional systems, far from mirroring the global regimes, have been able to go beyond what is universally agreed. The African Protocol on Violence Against Women is one such example. It has had influence over new legislation in Africa and represents a new approach to modern human rights problems. The ASEAN Declaration adopted by Brunei Darussalam, Cambodia, Indonesia, Laos, Malaysia, Myanmar, Philippines, Singapore, Thailand, and Viet Nam includes states that have been sceptical about whether human rights reflect their cultural outlook. The new Declaration, while it has been criticized for omitting certain rights, includes innovative clauses on human smuggling or trafficking in persons, including trafficking in human organs, protection for children from child labour, and a clause obligating ASEAN states to 'create a positive environment in overcoming stigma, silence, denial and discrimination in the prevention, treatment, care and support of people suffering from communicable diseases, including AIDs'. The human rights catalogue will continue to expand as new challenges emerge and new constituencies find it helpful to frame their claims as issues of human rights.

Chapter 3
Human rights foreign policy and the role of the United Nations

The narrative about agreed texts and their international supervision leaves many dissatisfied. Where is the enforcement of these rights? We have a legal framework and reports from international secretariats and non-governmental organizations, but where is the pressure to ensure that these rights are realized in practice? What does it really mean when governments say that their foreign policy is concerned with promoting and protecting human rights? Only very rarely do governments actually invoke these treaties before international courts in order to bring international complaints against other states. Clearly human rights discourse operates beyond the courtroom and can be an important element of foreign policy, but what does this mean in practical terms?

Foreign policy and the issue of non-interference

The idea that governments can legitimately concern themselves with the way in which another state treats its own nationals is a relatively recent innovation in international relations. The concept of non-interference in domestic affairs loomed large for much of the 20th century and meant that human rights were not a suitable topic for inclusion in foreign policy (see Box 15).

Box 15 Preface to *The Lawful Rights of Mankind* by Paul Sieghart

Down to the end of the second world war, it was a matter of universally accepted doctrine in international affairs that how a state treated its own citizens was a matter entirely for its own sovereign determination, and not the legitimate concern of anyone outside its own frontiers. Had a well-meaning delegation from abroad called on Chancellor Adolf Hitler in 1936 to complain about the notorious Nürnberg laws, and the manner in which they were being applied to persecute German Jews, the Führer would probably have dismissed such an initiative with the classic phrase of 'an illegitimate interference in the internal affairs of the sovereign German state', pointing out that these laws had been enacted in full accordance with the provisions of the German Constitution, by an assembly constitutionally and legally competent to enact them, and that neither they nor their application were the concern of meddling foreigners. And in international law as it then stood, he would have been perfectly right—and so would party Secretary-General Josef Stalin have been if a similar delegation had called upon him at around the same time to complain about the wholesale destruction of the kulaks in the Soviet Union.

Samuel Moyn's recent writing has sought to emphasize that, even if the Universal Declaration of Human Rights represented a watershed in terms of cataloguing human rights placing human rights above and beyond the national legal orders, it was not, according to him, until around 1977 that human rights 'exploded' onto the English speaking scene and played a significant role in the media and foreign policy of nations such as the United States (see Box 16).

Today several states have human rights units within their foreign offices, advisory committees on human rights, and even ministers

Box 16 S. Moyn, *The Last Utopia*

To be sure, there were a number of catalysts for the explosion: the search for a European identity outside Cold War terms; the reception of Soviet and later East European dissidents by politicians, journalists, and intellectuals; and the American liberal shift in foreign policy in new, moralized terms, after the Vietnamese disaster. Equally significant, but more neglected, were the end of formal colonialism and the crisis of the postcolonial state, certainly in the eyes of Western observers. The best general explanation for the origins of this social movement and common discourse around rights remains the collapse of other, prior utopias, both state-based and internationalist.

for human rights. The European Union has a Special Representative for Human Rights. Of course, there is a difference between proclaiming that human rights are at the heart of foreign policy, and actually changing the way decisions are taken. Respect for human rights is certainly now a factor to be considered in a number of spheres of inter-state decision making: admission to certain international and regional organizations; trade agreements and preferential tariffs; export credit guarantees; arms transfers; foreign direct investment; cooperation with international financial institutions; UN technical assistance programmes; development work; international investment agreements; customs communities; and the maintenance of international peace and security. The human rights record or reputation of a state can adversely affect any of these. A willingness to improve human rights has also almost become a condition for entering into a range of diverse arrangements with other states. One obvious example is that respect for human rights became a formal pre-condition for admission to the European Union and detailed demands were made on states such as Bulgaria and Croatia.

In contrast to this apparent progress, we must remind ourselves that promoting human rights in other countries still comes pretty low down the list of a government's priorities when there is a perceived clash with other competing 'national interests'. The extent to which this will change depends on the enthusiasm of people to hold their leaders to a human rights foreign policy that reorganizes these priorities.

One tension that deserves special consideration here is the question of potential arms transfers that could lead to serious violations of human rights. Although various states already have their own internal rules concerning arms transfers, the entry into force on 24 December 2014 of the new Arms Trade Treaty has now increased attention to the human rights implications of any potential arms transfer. The new Treaty prohibits any transfer where there is knowledge that the arms or items would be used in the commission of genocide, crimes against of humanity, or certain war crimes. Furthermore where there is an overriding risk that an export could be used to commit or facilitate a serious violation of human rights law, or the offence of trafficking in persons, then the export must not be authorized. Some of the top arms exporters have agreed to be bound by this treaty: France, Germany, Italy, Spain, and the United Kingdom. The United States has so far merely signed the treaty, but domestic preoccupation with the constitutional protection of the right to bear arms means that there will be opposition to joining this regime, even though the United States has fairly strict laws which are supposed to prevent arms transfers to those violating human rights (see Box 17).

The limits of human rights foreign policy

The promotion of human rights through foreign policy may be open to criticism on several grounds. First, there is the reaction from certain states which see a creeping justification for the use of military force. There was a sharp reaction from key states to the NATO bombing of Serbia in 1998 (in connection with Kosovo) and

Box 17 Amnesty International, 'Arms Trade Treaty Guide'

The USA is by far the world's largest arms trader, accounting for around 30 per cent of conventional arms transfers in terms of value. Its position on the [Arms Trade Treaty] is therefore key.

Key customers

The USA supplies arms to more than 170 countries. It has restricted arms transfers to Myanmar, China, Sri Lanka and Zimbabwe and countries subject to UN arms embargoes. However, it has supplied arms to countries including Iraq, Israel, Sri Lanka, Bahrain, Egypt and Yemen, where they have risked being used for serious human rights violations.

Irresponsible transfers

The USA is Egypt's and Israel's main arms supplier, selling major weapons as well as small arms, ammunition and chemical agents for riot control, despite the violent crackdown on protesters. The USA also supplied Yemen with small arms, chemical agents and armoured vehicles, and Bahrain with small arms. It provided Colombia's security forces with arms, military aid and training, despite their persistent human rights violations.

the NATO intervention over Libya in 2011, even though the latter was authorized by the Security Council. With regard to the latter intervention, the criticism from Russia and China arose from the fact that they considered the UK, France, and the USA had gone beyond their stated mission of protecting civilians. Russia and China felt that the intervention had been used to engineer regime change. Although there has been little enthusiasm for military intervention against the Syrian Government, despite the humanitarian and human rights crisis there, the emergence in 2014 of a vicious armed group, the self-styled 'Islamic state' (also known by the Arabic acronym DAESH), led not only to condemnations of human rights violations but also to limited air strikes on this group by the United States and others.

An assessment of any human rights-based justifications for the use of military force is complicated by the following factors. First, in many situations there will be a danger that the necessary force used to intervene could do more harm than good. People get killed in military interventions; how many deaths are justified in a bid to save lives? Even where human rights violations are actually ongoing, human rights activists have sometimes baulked at supporting the use of military force in the name of human rights (see Figure 7). The US-based organization Human Rights Watch wrote in its 2004 *World Report*:

> now that the war's proponents are relying so significantly on a humanitarian rationale for the war, the need to assess this claim has grown in importance. We conclude that, despite the horrors of Saddam Hussein's rule, the invasion of Iraq cannot be justified as a humanitarian intervention.

Another problem for human rights foreign policy is that governments resent being told what to do by states that themselves seem to have no respect for the rules. Today criticism by the United States is likely to be met with references to the infamous torture programme and network of secret transfers that was exposed as part of their 'war on terror'. The continued use of drone strikes for targeted killing, and the failure to deal with those still detained without trial in Guantánamo Bay, have made it hard for the United States to criticize the human rights records of other countries. Other states accused of human rights violations, or even complicity in the violations committed by the United States committed in the post-September 11 period, have also found it harder to take the moral high-ground.

The public human rights condemnations of the Cold War risk ringing hollow when the accused can counter with well-documented

7. 'No war in the name of human rights': a demonstration in Berne (Switzerland) against the 2003 Iraq war.

incidents of torture and abuse. More generally states accused of violating human rights remain protective of their reputations, and can make life difficult for those states that choose to embarrass them. The response to criticism can be non-cooperation in other fields (including those of trade and military assistance). Legislative reforms, which might otherwise have gone through, could be shelved in order to be seen to be defiantly refusing to bow to pressure. One 21st century response has been for foreign ministries to engage in private 'human rights dialogues' rather than public diplomatic denunciation. Of course the confidential nature of these dialogues makes it difficult to assess their effectiveness, but human rights organizations have not always seen them as a suitable substitute for a different sort of engagement. In an interview, Ken Roth from Human Rights Watch said:

> One illustration of the lack of seriousness of the private, backroom human rights 'dialogues' that many Western governments engage in with China is that they make little effort to speak to the Chinese public. Rather than emboldening domestic efforts for change, these quiet dialogues serve little purpose other than to enable Western leaders to pretend that their governments are addressing rights in China while avoiding the need to take up the issue themselves in a public way that might help to make a difference.

Clearly nearly all states will have to weigh speaking out on human rights against other interests. The extent to which a government does speak out will, however, be determined not only by the other interests at stake, but also by the strength of feeling among its people that human rights violations abroad should be denounced. The chances of bringing about an immediate end to human rights violations being committed in another state may be slim, but the delegitimizing effect on that state's regime may be significant, and the victims and civil society groups fighting to protect these rights at the local level may well feel emboldened.

Precisely because agitation from the bottom up can threaten existing power relations, we may be witnessing a renewed clampdown on foreign funding for non-governmental organizations. Several new laws limit the capacity of local organizations to receive foreign funding (see Box 18).

Box 18 *The Economist* (2014), 'Foreign funding of NGOs'

Azerbaijan, Mexico, Pakistan, Russia, Sudan and Venezuela have all passed laws in the past two years affecting NGOs that receive foreign funds. Around a dozen more countries plan to do so, including Bangladesh, Egypt, Malaysia and Nigeria. NGOs focused on democracy-building or human rights are the most affected, but the crackdown is also hitting those active in other areas, such as public health.

In the years following the cold war, some autocratic governments saw welcoming foreign support and cash for NGOs as an easy way to win favour with America and its allies. But the role played in Ukraine's 2004 Orange revolution by NGOs, including some that had received money from the Open Society Institute, which was founded by George Soros, an American billionaire, led to a change in attitude. The next year Vladimir Putin, Russia's president, declared that 'public organisations' could not receive foreign assistance; by 2012 NGOs that received money from abroad and engaged in 'political activities', broadly defined, had to register as 'foreign agents', a phrase that comes close to implying espionage.

This year, after NGOs refused to comply, Russia's government gave itself the power to deem them foreign agents by fiat. Last month the Soldiers' Mothers of St Petersburg, a group seeking information about Russian servicemen thought to have been injured or killed in Ukraine, was declared a foreign agent despite protestations that it receives no money from abroad.

Many of the new laws are broadly drafted and vague about the criteria for blocking foreign cash. Russian NGOs active in sensitive areas, such as human rights, have had their offices raided in the hunt for evidence of foreign influence. Uzbekistan requires all foreign donations to be paid into two state-owned banks,

In a way, today all states actually have a human rights foreign
policy to the extent that they participate in the human rights
debates at the United Nations, and it is to this subject that we
now turn.

Human rights and the UN today

Early on, the UN member states established a Committee
initially composed of nine individual members referred to as the
'nuclear Commission on Human Rights'. These individuals
proposed that the members of the future Commission should
'consist of highly qualified persons' and 'serve as non-governmental
representatives' and act as independent experts rather than
presenting the views of their governments. The governments
themselves rejected this proposal. The UN member states sitting
in the Commission's parent body decided that the new Human
Rights Commission should comprise representatives from
the eighteen member states that would make up the
new Commission.

The new Commission's agenda fluctuated over the years,
responding to the shifting balance of power between its member
states. The first years of the Commission's work focused on
standard setting, which it accomplished through the drafting of
the Universal Declaration and the International Covenants. With
the arrival of members from the developing world in the 1960s,
issues of racial discrimination in Southern Africa and the Israeli

occupation came to the forefront of the Commission's agenda. Following concern over the 1973 coup in Chile against the Socialist Government of President Allende, and the subsequent human rights violations in Chile and in Argentina, the Commission's agenda adapted in the 1980s to include public and confidential discussion of such country situations (see Figure 8).

The Commission developed a series of 'special procedures' for monitoring violations in selected countries, through individuals nominated to act either as country or thematic experts. These experts (also known as special rapporteurs) submit reports to the relevant UN bodies. They undertake country visits which are the subject of separate reports, and, in addition, they correspond with governments through 'urgent appeals' and 'letters of allegation'. These 'communications' allege human rights violations and generate some responses from governments. In 2013 this covered 1,520 individuals and the response rate was 45 per cent. Even

8. The Mothers of the Plaza de Mayo, who gathered weekly at the Plaza de Mayo in Buenos Aires to demand justice for their children who 'disappeared' during the Argentine military dictatorship between 1976 and 1983.

where the faxes, letters, and emails are ignored or dismissed, the process of putting governments on notice that the UN's watchdogs have been alerted has led to releases of those being detained and changes in policy. By any account, the work of these *pro-bono* human rights experts provides a remarkable tapestry of human rights information, analysis, and recommendations (see Box 19 for lists of the themes covered so far).

In 2006, the Commission was abolished and replaced with the Human Rights Council. Why did this happen? The perception had

Box 19 Thematic UN special procedures

Enforced or involuntary disappearances; extrajudicial, summary or arbitrary executions; torture and other cruel, inhuman or degrading treatment or punishment; freedom of religion or belief; mercenaries; sale of children, child prostitution and child pornography; arbitrary detention; internally displaced; racism and xenophobia; freedom of expression; right to development; violence against women; independence of judges and lawyers; structural adjustment policies and foreign debt; toxic and dangerous products and wastes; right to education; children in armed conflict; restitution, compensation and rehabilitation for victims; extreme poverty; migrants; right to food; adequate housing; human rights defenders; indigenous peoples; right to health; racial discrimination faced by people of African descent; human rights and counter-terrorism; minority issues; international solidarity; trafficking in persons; human rights and transnational corporations and other business enterprises; slavery; water and sanitation; cultural rights; discrimination against women; peaceful association and assembly; promotion of a democratic and equitable international order; truth, justice, reparation & guarantees on non-recurrence (transitional justice); sustainable environment; older persons; privacy, and human rights of persons with albinism.

started to grow in 2001 that a bloc of states had succeeded in shielding themselves and their allies from being condemned by the Commission, a Commission we might recall comprised of fifty-three representatives of states. It was alleged that governments were seeking election to the Commission in order to table procedural motions to block action and swap votes in order to insulate themselves from condemnation.

The UN body had become selective in its examination of country situations because the selection was being undertaken by the same governments that ought to be condemned. Commentators repeatedly pointed out, in a well-worn cliché, that the foxes were guarding the chicken coup.

The resulting reform was centred on making it more difficult for a government to get elected to this UN human rights body. The results have not been as significant as some would have hoped; but the fact is that some states, that might otherwise have succeeded, have failed to secure election under the new rules. Successful civil society campaigns were mounted in the face of candidacies from Sri Lanka and Belarus, while Syria and Sudan felt obliged to withdraw their candidacies.

One innovative feature of the new Human Rights Council deserves examination. A new procedure called 'Universal Periodic Review' (UPR) has been created. The Council now reviews every UN member state's compliance with all of its human rights obligations and commitments. This means that certain influential states can no longer escape scrutiny. Every state in the world is examined in meetings up to a total of over four and a half hours. For the cycle to cover the whole UN membership takes around four and a half years. Every state is entitled to pose questions and make recommendations to the state under review (although of course these are limited to interventions of a few minutes each). These recommendations and the replies by the relevant government officials of the state under review are now webcast.

While most of the exchanges are best described as 'diplomatic', and while some recommendations are more meaningful than others, the examination has become a springboard for follow-up action by non-governmental organizations, governments, and the UN itself.

Preliminary findings suggest that concrete steps have been taken towards greater engagement with the UN supervisory regimes, limited legal reform, and greater engagement with civil society. While states remain free to accept or reject recommendations, with this review procedure we have a significant shift away from the bloc politics of the previous years. Each recommendation is formulated by a single government and addressed to a single state or perhaps even a particular ministry. The expectation is that these hundreds of bilateral recommendations are followed up by all sides outside the ritualistic atmosphere of the actual review. Perhaps the most unremarked, but in the end remarkable, aspect of the process is that for each state under review there is a publicly available set of reports outlining the human rights issues faced by the state. These include not only the state's own report, but also a summary of the issues raised by non-governmental organizations and the UN's own reports. Taken together with the lists of recommendations, and the state's follow-up reports on implementation, this documentation provides a relatively accessible portrait of on-going human rights concerns for every country in the world.

Second, new rules make it considerably easier to call for special sessions of the UN body. Such sessions can be called at the initiative of one member with the support of one-third of the membership. In other words it is sufficient to garner sixteen votes out of forty-seven. The Council has held over twenty special sessions enabling human rights issues to be aired over a whole day. Interestingly the focus is no longer limited to governments, the Council recently condemned by consensus human rights violations committed by non-state actors such as the self-styled 'Islamic state' (see Figure 9 and Box 20) or, more recently, Boko Harem.

9. ISIS execution.

> **Box 20 'The human rights situation in Iraq in the light of abuses committed by the so-called Islamic State in Iraq and the Levant and associated groups', UN Human Rights Council, Resolution (2014)**
>
> *Condemns* in the strongest possible terms the systematic violations and abuses of human rights and violations of international humanitarian law resulting from the terrorist acts committed by the so-called Islamic State in Iraq and the Levant and associated groups taking place since 10 June 2014 in several provinces of Iraq, which may amount to war crimes and crimes against humanity, and strongly condemns in particular all violence against persons based on their religious or ethnic affiliation, as well as violence against women and children.

Of course politics plays a role whenever there are attempts to condemn a government. In such a situation there will inevitably be resistance, not only from the government under attack, but also from its allies who will be guarding against what are perceived to be issues of interference with sovereignty. Some states have been able to avoid criticism through diplomatic offensives or finding like-minded states to fend off such 'interference'. In the 2009 special session on Sri Lanka, the Council failed to condemn any violations by the government and simply encouraged it to continue cooperation with the UN. Subsequent UN reports into the situation painted a grim picture affecting hundreds of thousands of civilians and a failure by UN member states and UN officials to confront the government at the time. A different majority of the Council later took up the challenge and called for the High Commissioner for Human Rights to monitor the situation and undertake an investigation into 'alleged serious violations and abuses of human rights and related crimes by both parties in Sri Lanka' with a view to 'avoiding impunity and ensuring accountability'. Such Resolutions are divisive (see Figure 10) but have nevertheless re-established the Human Rights Council as a forum that addresses serious violations and establishes the sorts of investigations that can eventually lead to some sort of accountability.

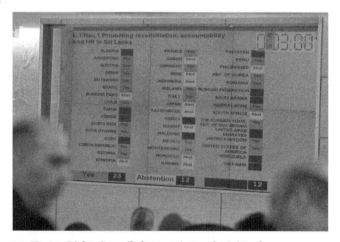

10. **Human Rights Council photo, voting on the Sri Lanka Resolution 2014, yes 23, abstentions 12, no 12.**

Perhaps just as significant is the way that the Council's actions stimulate follow-up and scrutiny outside the formal set piece sessions. The *Universal Periodic Review* (UPR) described earlier in this chapter is essentially a series of bilateral exchanges between states. After the session some governments that made recommendations will follow these up through their embassies in the state under review and genuinely seek improvements. One should judge the efficacy of the Review neither by the public exchanges conducted for the benefit of the webcam, nor by how many recommendations are formally accepted or rejected, but rather by the human rights improvements actually instigated by the state under review. Some states have been quite comprehensive in publishing the steps they have taken, or not taken, to respond to recommendations. This has extended to what are now known as 'mid-term reports' with one non-governmental organization (UPR Info) conducting 'mid-term implementation assessments'. The early results suggest that some steps are indeed taken (see Box 21) and that civil society is, in some situations, being taken more seriously and enjoying greater access to policy making. The challenge will be to keep the process inclusive, concrete, and meaningful.

The danger at the UN today, is not so much that debates degenerate into ideological slanging matches or the politics of the bloc, rather the problem is that there is a temptation to waste time praising like-minded governments that could benefit from a rather more honest critical approach. The price of effectiveness will be constant vigilance against UPR becoming a 'Universal Praise Review'. Walter Kälin highlights the dangers of UPR descending into ritualism on both sides: 'it provides states that have a weak human rights record and low commitment with an opportunity to claim they are dedicated to human rights simply by virtue of participation in the UPR and accepting recommendations.' And he sees ritualism on the side of the recommending state when their diplomats no longer study the human rights situation in the country under review 'but regularly make the same (weak) recommendations'.

Box 21 UPR Info, 'Beyond Promises'

Issues such as women's rights, international instruments, and children's rights had the overall highest number of recommendations that triggered action, but the issues with the highest percentage of implementation within the issue categories were HIV-Aids, human trafficking, and people with disabilities. Alternatively, the highest percentages of non-implementation within categories were of recommendations pertaining to the freedom of movement, right to land, and the death penalty.

With the information derived from the [mid-term implementation assessments], we now know that action was triggered by mid-term for 48 per cent of the recommendations for which we received comments (over 11,500 recommendations). This means that 48 per cent of recommendations were either partially or fully implemented 2.5 years after the review. Real progress was illustrated for a wide variety of vulnerable groups: children, minorities, women, people with disabilities, and many more. The potential of the UPR is yet to be fully exploited, but stakeholders are continuously learning from their experiences and perfecting their approaches.

The media focus on the output of UN bodies such as the Council. But to concentrate on the behaviour of diplomats at the United Nations is to overlook much of the UN's activity on human rights. In addition to the UN's monitoring of states through the expert treaty bodies and the special procedures, the UN has expanded its attention to human rights in further important contexts. First, a number of UN field operations have been established with a human rights role. Such operations are mandated to offer protection, monitor the situation, and offer assistance. These operations, together with peace operations mandated to protect civilians, have enjoyed some success in implementing human rights protection and achieving improvements on the ground. Second, the UN programmes and funds that deal with issues such as children, women, health, and development have started to use human rights principles to underpin their work.

Occasionally, the UN is even able to go beyond what the member states have explicitly agreed to do and say. We can detect here a sort of 'supranational' approach to human rights. The UN Secretary-General, the UN High Commissioner for Human Rights, the Human Rights Commissioner for the Council of Europe, and other senior figures from the secretariats of international and regional organizations can operate in ways that extend beyond simply fulfilling the tasks set by a particular group of governments. They can speak up and speak out when governments are unwilling to do so. Much depends on the determination of the individuals recruited by the relevant inter-governmental organization.

To illustrate the point let us consider the following episode. Mary Robinson, as the UN High Commissioner for Human Rights, issued a statement on Chechnya expressing concern about the fact that 'indiscriminate and disproportionate use of force is causing high civilian loss of life and injuries'. At the inter-state level at that time, no inter-governmental body could summon a majority to voice a similar level of concern or take concrete action. It is telling that even the United States, which has a stated human rights foreign policy, will at times distinguish its approach from that of the UN High Commissioner for Human Rights. Governments may feel the need to 'pull their punches' in terms of lecturing other countries on how to behave or protesting violations of human rights by another country's security forces. On a tour of Africa by the US Secretary of State, the *New York Times* reported one member of the party as stating: 'We don't do Mary Robinson.' The report continues 'an allusion to UN High Commissioner for Human Rights, who has no other agenda. In Africa today, the United States has many other interests, including the promotion of stability and security, which often means the use of methods not appreciated by human rights groups.'

The fact that a UN programme such as the Office of the High Commissioner for Human Rights has no strategic military or trade interests, means that there is a possibility that human rights issues will be raised when this would otherwise be precluded by foreign policy considerations (even in a body like the Human Rights Council which is supposed to be a forum for airing such issues). Of course, the Office of the High Commissioner for Human Rights will feel that it has to work within the parameters of what is acceptable to governments or risk losing budget, cooperation, and support. But the Office has created some room to develop its own voice and ought to be expected to articulate concern, even outrage, at human rights violations wherever they occur. Over the last twenty years the Office has grown in size and ambition. It now has over 500 personnel at its headquarters in Geneva, and about 1,350 personnel around the world in field presences, peace operations, and political missions. The Office's annual budget is around $200 million.

Chapter 4
Torture

As we saw in Chapter 3, some human rights violations give rise
to individual criminal responsibility at the international level.
This creates not only obligations for governments to investigate
and prosecute, but also means that people can be arrested and
prosecuted outside their own country. We have already referred
to war crimes and set out the definitions of genocide and crimes
against humanity. Such crimes have sometimes been prosecuted
in international tribunals and, on occasion, at the national level.
The crime we shall now consider is torture. The prohibition on
torture in the UN Convention against Torture is described in
absolute terms: 'No exceptional circumstances whatsoever, whether
a state of war or a threat of war, internal political instability or
any other public emergency, may be invoked as a justification of
torture.' But we know that torture unfortunately still goes on
around the world. To better understand the challenges involved,
it is worth recalling a little of the history of torture.

The purposes of torture have been various. In some contexts
torture was considered a useful way to extract confessions and
provide essential proof for a conviction at trial. Although the
English common law prohibited torture, an exceptional procedure
allowed the King to issue 'torture warrants' through the Star
Chamber. One of the most famous individuals subjected to this
procedure was Guy Fawkes, caught trying to blow up the Houses

of Parliament in 1605. He was tortured into giving up the names of his accomplices (see Box 22). However, this form of investigation became seen as emblematic of the abuse of power by the King, it was therefore abolished, along with the Star Chamber, in 1640. Although the Roman-Canon law tradition in Continental Europe continued to accept confessions extracted by torture as providing useful elements of proof, this practice was increasingly seen, not only as unreliable, but also as unfair to the innocent.

In modern times we have seen how brutal regimes have considered that torture would remind dissidents and the general population who was in charge—and determined to remain in charge. In the 1970s, an anti-torture campaign, led by groups such as Amnesty International, was successful in highlighting torture, developing the norm, focusing on the criminal aspect, and

Box 22 Lord Hope, *A v Secretary of State for the Home Department* (2005)

Four hundred years ago, on 4 November 1605, Guy Fawkes was arrested when he was preparing to blow up the Parliament which was to be opened the next day, together with the King and all the others assembled there. Two days later James I sent orders to the Tower authorising torture to be used to persuade Fawkes to confess and reveal the names of his co-conspirators. His letter stated that 'the gentler tortours' were first to be used on him, and that his torturers were then to proceed to the worst until the information was extracted out of him. On 9 November 1605 he signed his confession with a signature that was barely legible and gave the names of his fellow conspirators. On 27 January 1606 he and seven others were tried before a special commission in Westminster Hall. Signed statements in which they had each confessed to treason were shown to them at the trial, acknowledged by them to be their own and then read to the jury.

instituting monitoring mechanisms. Building on the work done in exposing torture during the Greek regime, the campaign galvanized a public beyond the cautious diplomats at the Human Rights Commission. A first signature on the petition appealing to the UN General Assembly was from singer Joan Baez, who promoted the petition at her 1973 concert in London. The petition eventually gathered over a million signatures and generated engagement by citizens who brought pressure on their governments to adopt the demanded declaration at the UN General Assembly. The campaign worked with technical governmental committees concerned with crime and medical ethics, thereby co-opting different constituencies beyond the world of human rights as foreign policy.

The eventual Declaration was adopted in 1975 'as a guideline for all States and other entities exercising effective Power.' Although states were expected to make torture and complicity in torture offences under national law, the Declaration stopped short of addressing torture as an issue of international criminal law. It took another decade before states adopted the 1984 *Convention against Torture and Other Cruel, Inhuman or Degrading Treatment or Punishment* which demanded that a state where an alleged torturer is found is obliged to extradite or submit the case to its prosecutors. In effect this internationalized the criminal prosecution of torture elevating this human rights violation into the realm of international criminal law.

Senator Pinochet's arrest and detention in London resulted from the application of the rules contained in this Convention and, more recently, we have seen this treaty used by the British Courts to override claims of immunity in the face of allegations of torture levelled against Prince Al Khalifa, Commander of the Royal Guard of the Kingdom of Bahrain. The treaty also provided the context for the arrest in Senegal of the former President of Chad, Hissène Habré, with a view to his eventual prosecution for crimes of torture. Furthermore, in 2005, the Afghan rebel leader,

Faryadi Zardad, was convicted at the Old Bailey in London of torture and hostage-taking and sentenced to twenty years' imprisonment; and in 2009 a US Court sentenced 'Chuckie' Taylor (son of the former President of Liberia) to ninety-seven years in prison for offences of torture. These cases have become reminders that, even if only a few leaders involved with torture are ever arrested and tried abroad, past human rights violations can catch up with anyone in the end. Most recently, in 2012–14, we saw hundreds of Argentinean former officials tried for torture, kidnapping, and murder during the regime of the *Junta* (1976 to 1983). Many have been sentenced to life in prison, including those prosecuted for their role in the *centros clandestinos de detención tortura y exterminio* (secret centres for detention, torture, and extermination).

Torture in the 'war on terror'

Let us now see how the absolute prohibition of torture has come under strain in recent times. First, in the wake of the shocking September 11 attacks on the United States in 2001, there were attempts to define torture in a particularly narrow way. The interpretation of the term in a 2002 memorandum of the US Justice Department read torture so narrowly as to amount to the intentional infliction of 'excruciating' or 'agonizing' pain. A series of policies set the scene for what has become known as the torture programme and multiple incidents of prisoner abuse. Other memos suggested that the Constitutional prohibition against torture did not apply to alien enemy combatants abroad, and that the President could 'override' international law. When the photos of abused Iraqi prisoners surfaced, providing graphic evidence of the humiliation being meted out, many blamed the policy makers as well as the disgraced prison guards (see Figure 11).

The scandal shocked politicians from both parties, and, on coming to Office, President Obama immediately repudiated all these

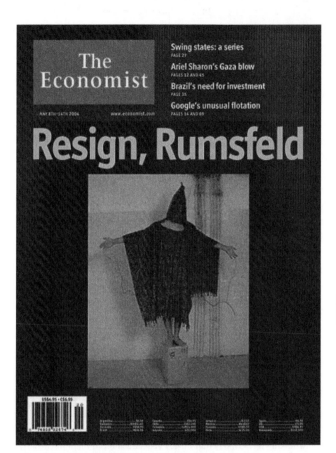

11. Images of the abuse and humiliation of Iraqi prisoners were flashed around the world. The photo of the hooded man on a box with electrical wires became emblematic of the human rights abuses committed against prisoners in Iraq.

previous memos. He later explained why torture was not only ineffective, but also counterproductive, due to the violence it engendered against US personnel in Iraq and Afghanistan. Obama nevertheless suggested that he believed that 'we need to look forward as opposed to looking backwards', and the

Administration later concluded that there was insufficient evidence to prosecute CIA interrogators. The eventual publication in 2014 by the Senate's Select Committee on Intelligence of a redacted version of a summary of a report into the CIA's detention and interrogation programme triggered a vigorous debate which seemed to focus on whether the CIA programme had actually provided useful information. The issue of whether or not the programme produced useful intelligence has, for the most part, displaced any discussion about prosecuting the perpetrators. Respect for human rights means that all forms of torture, inhuman or degrading treatment are strictly prohibited. It matters not whether this can lead to information, even if the information might be seen as the only way to disarm a 'ticking time bomb'.

In a speech given on 21st May 2009, President Obama said:

I know some have argued that brutal methods like waterboarding were necessary to keep us safe. I could not disagree more. As Commander-in-Chief, I see the intelligence. I bear the responsibility for keeping this country safe. And I categorically reject the assertion that these are the most effective means of interrogation. What's more, they undermine the rule of law. They alienate us in the world. They serve as a recruitment tool for terrorists, and increase the will of our enemies to fight us, while decreasing the will of others to work with America. They risk the lives of our troops by making it less likely that others will surrender to them in battle, and more likely that Americans will be mistreated if they are captured. In short, they did not advance our war and counterterrorism efforts—they undermined them, and that is why I ended them once and for all.

Other states such as Canada and the United Kingdom have found themselves accused of assisting or condoning the torture techniques that were being developed by the United States and other states in their interrogation of suspects in their 'war on terror'. The United Kingdom issued guidance on what personnel should do when they consider there is a risk of torture or cruel inhuman or degrading treatment taking place 'at the hands of third parties'. The Guidance also details prohibited forms of treatment (see Box 23).

Box 23 UK Guidance on Interviewing Detainees and the Passing and Receipt of Information, 2010

Torture

An offence under UK law, torture is defined as a public official intentionally inflicting severe mental or physical pain or suffering in the performance or purported performance of his duties.

Cruel, inhuman or degrading treatment or punishment

Cruel, Inhuman or Degrading Treatment or Punishment (CIDT) is a term which is used in some international treaties but is not defined in UK law. In the context of this guidance, the UK Government considers that the following practices, which is not an exhaustive list, could constitute cruel, inhuman or degrading treatment or punishment:

(i) use of stress positions;

(ii) sleep deprivation;

(iii) methods of obscuring vision (except where these do not pose a risk to the detainee's physical or mental health and is necessary for security reasons during arrest or transit) and hooding;

(iv) physical abuse or punishment of any sort;

(v) withdrawal of food, water or medical help;

(vi) degrading treatment (sexual embarrassment, religious taunting etc); and

(vii) deliberate use of 'white' or other noise.

Information gleaned from torture

Today, the purpose of coercive treatment is no longer really about obtaining a confession for trial, as happened for Guy Fawkes, it being widely acknowledged that few legal systems would accept that evidence procured through such methods should be admitted in court. The purpose is said to be to gather intelligence about the terrorist network and to prevent future attacks. This brings us back to the ticking time bomb scenario which asks: might some incidents of torture or ill-treatment be justified to avert a terrorist attack? The media never tire of presenting this dilemma for the protagonists in action films, and the former Directors of the CIA in 2014 very publicly invoked this scenario to justify the CIA's actions in the wake of September 11.

The argument that the torture of a few individuals could save the lives of many innocents is repeatedly rehearsed. Several counter-arguments have been developed. First, it is said that information produced under torture is unreliable as the victim will say anything to avoid the pain. Therefore, torture is more likely to generate false leads than help any investigation. Second, it is argued that once allowed in exceptional circumstances, the use of torture will spread, and we will find ourselves on a 'slippery slope' where mistreatment is seen as normal, even expected. Third, it is suggested that torture is simply wrong in any circumstance because it negates the whole idea that society exists to ensure that we all respect each other's worth or dignity.

But even after all the arguments for and against have been played out and torture has been officially outlawed, the idea of justifiable torture sneaks back into the contemporary discourse in the form of the suggestion by some that one could admit a possible defence of 'necessity' in the context of a criminal trial of a torturer. This was the view of the Israeli Supreme Court in 1999 when it declared that the General Security Service had no authority to use certain physical interrogation techniques such as shaking. In a parallel development when police officers were found to have threatened torture in order to get a suspect to reveal the whereabouts of an abducted child, a German Court chose to accept as mitigating circumstances the intention of the torturer to save life, and consequently imposed a caution and a suspended fine rather than any harsher measures (see Box 24 for further details).

Box 24 'Bad Torture—Good Torture?', by Florian Jessberger

On 27 September 2002, law student Magnus Gaefgen kidnapped 11-year-old Jakob von Metzler, the son of a senior bank executive, killed him in his apartment and hid the dead body close to a lake near Frankfurt. In accordance with his plan, he forwarded a letter to the boy's family in which he demanded one million Euros in return for the release of the child. Three days after the boy's disappearance, Gaefgen was arrested after being observed picking up the ransom. During his interrogation, the suspect gave evasive or misleading answers concerning his involvement in the abduction and provided no information about the whereabouts or health status of the boy. Finally, the day after the arrest, Frankfurt Police Vice-President, Wolfgang Daschner, who was responsible for the investigation, ordered that pain be inflicted on the suspect, without causing injuries, under medical supervision and subject to prior warning, in order to save the life of the boy. Accordingly, a subordinate police officer told Gaefgen, who was still in police custody, that the police were prepared to inflict pain on him that 'he would never forget' if he continued to withhold information concerning the whereabouts of the boy. Under the influence of this threat, Gaefgen gave full particulars of the whereabouts of the boy. The actual infliction of pain, which in fact had been arranged by fetching a specially trained

Box 24 Continued

police officer, was not necessary. Shortly thereafter, police officers found the body of the boy....

The judgment concluded that the act was neither justified nor excused, and that both defendants were criminally responsible.

However, the Court found 'massive mitigating circumstances' in favour of both defendants. The judgment referred in particular to the defendants' aim of saving the life of the child, but also mentioned the provocative behaviour of the suspect during the interrogations, a hectic atmosphere, great emotional pressure on the investigating officers, and the consequences of the crimes for the defendants, particularly the public attention the incident received.

Recent Canadian Guidance on this point seems to accept the idea that information derived from torture might in rare cases have to be legitimately shared in the face of a serious threat to life or property. The Ministerial Discretion to the Canadian Security Intelligence Service (2011) states:

> In exceptional circumstances, CSIS may need to share the most complete information in its possession, including information from foreign entities that was likely derived through mistreatment [torture or other cruel, inhuman, or degrading treatment or punishment], in order to mitigate a serious threat of loss of life, injury, or substantial damage or destruction of property before it materializes. In such rare circumstances, ignoring such information solely because of its source would represent an unacceptable risk to public safety.

All of this tells us that officials cannot bring themselves to actually authorize torture. No judges are today ready to find arguments to justify torture. This is not just because torture is forbidden under human rights law—something deeper is surely at stake. Quite why the prohibition is so absolute may depend on different ways of seeing the issue. For some, it is simply revolting and unacceptable to treat another human being in a way that is so obviously inhuman; for others, it denies the idea that we have a society and any meaningful sense of law that can protect us from one another. For many, it seems that, even if we accept that in the equation between some temporary pain and preventive life-saving action, the balance may come down in favour of some pain, the wise course is to avoid torture at all times for it risks expanding into general abuse for all sorts of prisoners—generating further resentment and violence aimed at the very population which the torturers seek to protect or save. None of these arguments, however, will convince someone who believes that lives could be saved by using a bit of rough treatment (or torture). And, as we have just seen, some legal systems have found ways to protect those who carry out this dirty work in the name of protecting the lives of others.

Politicians and indeed those responsible for these programmes have felt it appropriate to balance the well-being of the torture victim against the prospect of saving lives. Such an approach does not fit with the current understanding of the absolute ban on torture. Indeed, adherence to the outright ban reveals the extent of our commitment to the underlying values that inform human rights. In the end, I would suggest that it is our twin commitments to democracy and human dignity that underlie the continuing outright prohibition of torture. In the words of the political philosopher Steven Lukes:

> torture is doubly vicious, combining the vice of concealment and the vice of violence—specifically violence against the defenceless. The first is anti-democratic, preventing us from reaching a collective judgment; the second is anti-liberal, constituting, if anything does, a violation of dignity of a person.

The secondary rule that prohibits the use of evidence gleaned from torture has been the focus of a number of recent controversies and reveals how far we are prepared to go to stamp out torture and other forms of mistreatment. As already stated, no one really expects to use evidence extracted through torture to convict those accused of terrorism or kidnapping. The issue that has arisen is whether such information obtained through torture can be used, not for conviction, but for the continuing detention of terrorist suspects. At the end of 2005, the UK House of Lords delivered a landmark judgment holding that evidence resulting from torture could not be used in proceedings reviewing the legality of the detention of suspected terrorists.

There remain differences of opinion about what happens outside the courtroom. Some consider that the security services and the police executive should be able to rely on this information, as it could be essential to the protection of public safety (see Box 25). Prohibiting the use by anyone of any such information is said by some to be unrealistic when lives are at stake, and yet this only seems to encourage the use of torture or other inhuman treatment. The European Court of Human Rights was faced with this conundrum when they dealt with complaints brought by the convicted German law student (mentioned earlier in this chapter) who had been threatened with torture and then revealed the whereabouts of his victim. He claimed not only that he had been subjected to torture and inhuman treatment but that his trial had been unfair as the Court had relied on evidence gleaned from torture. The Court agreed that the threats amounted to inhuman treatment and that the lenient punishment handed out by the German authorities meant that Germany remained responsible. But the Court stopped short of ruling the trial unfair. Although the Court realized that a key way to prevent mistreatment is to prevent the authorities from using at trial any information that results from such treatment, in this case a majority of eleven judges felt they could distinguish between cases where the inhuman treatment had an impact on the conviction or sentence,

Box 25 Lord Rodger of Earlsferry in *A and others v Home Secretary* (2005)

Information obtained by torture may be unreliable. But all too often it will be reliable and of value to the torturer and his masters. That is why torturers ply their trade. Sadly, the Gestapo rolled up resistance networks and wiped out their members on the basis of information extracted under torture. Hence operatives sent to occupied countries were given suicide pills to prevent them from succumbing to torture and revealing valuable information about their mission and their contacts. In short, the torturer is abhorred as a *hostis humani generis* not because the information he produces may be unreliable but because of the barbaric means he uses to extract it.

The premise of this appeal is that, despite the United Nations Convention against Torture and any other obligations under international law, some states still practise torture. More than that, those states may supply information based on statements obtained under torture to the British security services who may find it useful in unearthing terrorist plots. Moreover, when issuing a certificate under section 21 of the 2001 Act, the Secretary of State may have to rely on material that includes such statements.

Mr Starmer QC, who appeared for Amnesty and a number of other interveners, indicated that, in their view, it would be wrong for the Home Secretary to rely on such statements since it would be tantamount to condoning the torture by which the statements were obtained. That stance has the great virtue of coherence; but the coherence is bought at too dear a price. It would mean that the Home Secretary might have to fail in one of the first duties of government, to protect people in this country from potential attack.

> **Box 26 European Court of Human Rights, Case of**
> ***Gäfgen v Germany*, 2010**
>
> [T]he failure to exclude the impugned real evidence, secured
> following a statement extracted by means of inhuman treatment,
> did not have a bearing on the applicant's conviction and sentence.
> As the applicant's defence rights and his right not to incriminate
> himself have likewise been respected, his trial as a whole must be
> considered to have been fair.

> **Box 27 European Court of Human Rights, Case of**
> ***Gäfgen v Germany*, 2010: dissenting opinion**
>
> Societies that are founded upon the rule of law do not tolerate
> or sanction, whether directly, indirectly or otherwise, the
> perpetration of treatment that is absolutely prohibited by Article
> 3 of the Convention.... Neither 'a break in the causal chain' nor
> any other intellectual construct can overcome the inherent
> wrong that occurs when evidence obtained in violation of Article
> 3 is admitted into criminal proceedings.

and those where there had been a 'break in the causal chain'.
In this case the Court determined that the trial was fair as the
evidence which resulted from the ill-treatment was not used to
prove him guilty (see Box 26). A minority of six judges felt such a
conclusion was retrogressive step and failed to take mistreatment
seriously (see Box 27).

Transfers for torture

Lastly, let us address the rule that prohibits sending anyone to
a country where they run a real risk of being tortured. Here
again there is universal agreement on the principle. But in its
application we see countervailing forces at work. Asylum-seekers

claim they will be tortured on return, immigration authorities question the available evidence, doubt the risk of future torture, and refer to 'diplomatic assurances' from the destination state that torture will not take place. A few well-known cases attest to genuine concern from human rights bodies that the practice of believing diplomatic assurances has led to violations of human rights. As we see in the next paragraph taken from the UN Committee Against Torture's Decision in *Agiza v Sweden*:

> 13.4 The Committee considers at the outset that it was known, or should have been known, to the State party's authorities at the time of the complainant's removal that Egypt resorted to consistent and widespread use of torture against detainees, and that the risk of such treatment was particularly high in the case of detainees held for political and security reasons.... The procurement of diplomatic assurances, which, moreover, provided no mechanism for their enforcement, did not suffice to protect against this manifest risk.

UN High Commissioner for Human Rights, Louise Arbour, chose to mark Human Rights Day with a statement about torture. She specifically challenged the practice of 'diplomatic assurances':

> There are many reasons to be sceptical about the value of those assurances. If there is no risk of torture in a particular case, they are unnecessary and redundant. If there is a risk, how effective are these assurances likely to be? Assurances that the death penalty will not be sought or imposed are easy to monitor. Not so, I suggest, in the case of torture and ill-treatment. Short of very intrusive and sophisticated monitoring measures, such as around-the-clock video surveillance of the deportee, there is little oversight that could guarantee that the risk of torture will be obliterated in any particular case. While detainees as a group may denounce their torturers if interviewed privately and anonymously, a single individual is unlikely to reveal his ill-treatment if he is to remain under the control of his tormentors after the departure of the 'monitors'.

Chapter 5
Deprivations of life and liberty

The absolute rights discussed so far do not allow for limitations, exceptions, qualifications, or balancing against other rights. Genocide, crimes against humanity, slavery, and torture are simply international crimes, which are prohibited at all times and can normally be punished by any state wherever the acts were committed. The rights we consider in this chapter may, by contrast, be limited through legal restrictions designed to protect a defined legitimate objective. So, for example, liberty can be restricted in the context of the detention of someone following a lawful conviction in a court of law. Freedom of speech is also not absolute. As we all know, shouting 'fire' in a crowded theatre can be punished. Although we all should have freedom of expression and the rights to receive and impart information, there may be legitimate restrictions on communicating for example commercial or military secrets. Photographs of celebrities may be of interest to a wide readership but certain images may be restricted in order to protect an individual's privacy. My right to information about you on the Internet clashes with the new so-called 'right to be forgotten' (we will look at this new right in more detail in Chapter 6).

Is it meaningful then to talk about 'rights' in such contexts? You have the right not be detained—until the authorities justify your detention. You have the right to publish—but not if it upsets others. We seem to be merely giving with one hand and taking away with the other. However, the human rights framework applies and is useful. The human rights approach starts from a presumption that we all have rights to liberty, fair trial, freedom of expression, belief, assembly, association, and property. Any restriction on these rights has to be justified as proportionate to the aims pursued by the restriction according to a four-stage schema developed in human rights law (examined under the heading 'Proportionality' in Chapter 6). The restriction on our freedoms need not be sinister or nefarious; few contest the need for certain convicted criminals to be deprived of their liberty. Introducing human rights in this context enables us to see how we have to start from the presumption that the individual is entitled to liberty unless a fair procedure demonstrates the necessity of incarceration.

The right to life

Let us start with the right to life and return to detention in the second part of this chapter. The right to life would seem at first glance to be absolute, but on closer inspection, it is clear that some deliberate acts which result in the loss of life are not necessarily human rights violations. A police officer, confronted by an armed assailant, may have to shoot in self-defence to save his or her own life or the lives of others. The cases become harder when the danger becomes less imminent. What if a state engages in the targeted assassination of suspected terrorists? Human rights courts have been faced with dozens of complaints that security forces have used excessive force in given circumstances. As a general rule, the force used has to be 'proportionate' to the danger to be averted. The UN *Basic Principles on the Use of Force and Firearms by Law Enforcement Officials* state that:

> Law enforcement officials shall not use firearms against persons except in self-defence or defence of others against the imminent threat of death or serious injury, to prevent the perpetration of a

particularly serious crime involving grave threat to life, to arrest a person presenting such a danger and resisting their authority, or to prevent his or her escape, and only when less extreme means are insufficient to achieve these objectives. In any event, intentional lethal use of firearms may only be made when strictly unavoidable in order to protect life.

This simple rule is under strain as governments seek to shift from the context of principles appropriate for confronting an armed robber or a hostage situation, to the realm of anticipatory self-defence to prevent attacks on the nation. This is sometimes attempted by adjusting the vocabulary and controlling the concepts. Instead of 'law enforcement' one is said to be dealing with a 'global war'; protecting life becomes protecting the nation; imminent threats are understood as continuous threats; criminals become international terrorists or 'unlawful enemy belligerents'. Of course there are rules that regulate killing in times of war, but the details of these rules were mostly designed for wars between the regular armed forces of two states. In such cases, and even in some civil wars, there is relative clarity concerning who constitute the armed forces and what constitute civilian objects. But targeting individual terrorists under cover of such rules is controversial. Some would say that the state should have to show that this targeted individual is actually playing a role in the attacks or even in an imminent attack. And then further questions arise: what sort of role? The person who is actually planting the bomb or the person on the look-out? Is the person who funds or shelters the alleged terrorist playing a role?

These controversies have come into sharp relief in the use of drones and the policy of targeted killings away from the battlefield. Drones are increasingly used out of convenience or where the use of force would otherwise be too risky or complicated. They are being manufactured and sold at a rate which suggests that the prospect of their use will be hovering for many years to come. While such 'unmanned aerial vehicles' may be more accurate than alternatives, they are also more easy to deploy where a state has no control of territory and so some of this killing now happens in new situations beyond the traditional theatre of armed conflict. In such situations, unlike a traditional confrontation on the battlefield, the unmanned aerial vehicle cannot yet accept a surrender and detain the target. The alternative of capture is no longer an alternative if counter-terrorsim is pursued through drone strikes.

As just suggested, the rules which the United States says it applies blur the edges between the established categories of law regulating when law-enforcement officials can use lethal force to avert an imminent killing, when states can use force against the armed forces of other states, and when armed forces can target military objectives in a war. Public concern has grown over the lack of transparency over who is being targeted, and on what grounds. The US Administration's policies were revealed in a White House Fact Sheet and leaked official White Paper (see Box 28). While these texts may have reassured some people, others remain concerned that serious questions remain: How

Box 28 White House Fact Sheet: Standards and Procedures for the Use of Force in Counterterrorism Operations Outside the United States and Areas of Active Hostilities

The policy of the United States is not to use lethal force when it is feasible to capture a terrorist suspect, because capturing a terrorist offers the best opportunity to gather meaningful intelligence and to mitigate and disrupt terrorist plots.

Lethal force will be used only to prevent or stop attacks against U.S. persons, and even then, only when capture is not feasible and no other reasonable alternatives exist to address the threat effectively.

Box 28 Continued

[L]ethal force will be used outside areas of active hostilities only when...

First, there must be a legal basis for using lethal force, whether it is against a senior operational leader of a terrorist organization or the forces that organization is using or intends to use to conduct terrorist attacks.

Second, the United States will use lethal force only against a target that poses a continuing, imminent threat to U.S. persons. It is simply not the case that all terrorists pose a continuing, imminent threat to U.S. persons; if a terrorist does not pose such a threat, the United States will not use lethal force.

Third, the following criteria must be met before lethal action may be taken:

1) Near certainty that the terrorist target is present;
2) Near certainty that non-combatants(*) will not be injured or killed;
3) An assessment that capture is not feasible at the time of the operation;
4) An assessment that the relevant governmental authorities in the country where action is contemplated cannot or will not effectively address the threat to U.S. persons; and
5) An assessment that no other reasonable alternatives exist to effectively address the threat to U.S. persons.

*Non-combatants are individuals who may not be made the object of attack under applicable international law. The term 'non-combatant' does not include an individual who is part of a belligerent party to an armed conflict, an individual who is taking a direct part in hostilities, or an individual who is targetable in the exercise of national self-defense. Males of military age may be non-combatants; it is not the case that all military-aged males in the vicinity of a target are deemed to be combatants.

Leaked US White Paper on Lawfulness of a Lethal Operation against a U.S. Citizen

A high-level official could conclude, for example, that an individual poses an 'imminent threat' of violent attack against the United States where he is an operational leader of al-Qa'ida or an associated force and is personally and continually involved in planning terrorist attacks against the United States. Moreover, where the al-Qa'ida member in question has recently been involved in activities posing an imminent threat of violent attack against the United States, and there is no evidence suggesting that he has renounced or abandoned such activities, that member's involvement in al-Qa'ida's continuing terrorist campaign against the United States would support the conclusion that the member poses an imminent threat.

imminent is imminent? What is a reasonable alternative? Who exactly is a non-combatant? Furthermore the associated problems remain: who controls the drone? Who takes the decision to put someone on the kill list? Will the strike simply recruit more warriors/terrorists?

It is striking that references to human rights and human dignity are absent from such legal justifications. This could be because some of the governments relying on such reasoning argue that human rights have no place on the battlefield, and that any killing should be dealt with under the laws of war. Three relevant rules are reproduced in Box 29. Additionally some governments argue that they have no human rights obligations when they operate abroad; but such reasoning sits uneasily with the idea that human beings are to be respected because each one of us has a *worth*. In a detailed study of the applicable human rights law, the UN

Special Rapporteur, Philip Alston, reaffirmed that outside armed conflict lethal force: 'is legal if it is strictly and directly necessary to save life.'

Detention

The human rights movement has often concerned itself with those who have been detained for their politics or expressing their opinion. Recall the symbolism attributed to the figure of Solzhenitsyn by Kundera in Chapter 1. The founding of Amnesty International in 1961 was prompted by its founder, the barrister Peter Benenson, reading about two Portuguese students publicly raising their glasses in a toast to freedom and then being convicted and sentenced to seven years' imprisonment. *The Observer* newspaper carried Benenson's 'Appeal for Amnesty' under the banner headline, 'The Forgotten Prisoners' (see Figure 12). The article included photographs of six prisoners: Constantin Noica (a Romanian philosopher); the civil rights supporter, Reverend Ashton from the United States; the Angolan poet, Agostinho

12. *The Observer* announces the Appeal for Amnesty, 28 May 1961. The overwhelming public response led to the eventual founding of Amnesty International.

Neto (held by the Portuguese); Archbishop Beran of Prague; Toni Ambatielos (a trade unionist detained in Greece); and Cardinal Mindszenty of Hungary (taking refuge in the US Embassy in Budapest). Other prisoners from Spain and South Africa were included in the article. The original Appeal for Amnesty had four aims: to work impartially for the release of those imprisoned for their opinions; to seek for them a fair and public trial; to enlarge the right of asylum and help political refugees to find work; and to urge effective international machinery to guarantee freedom of opinion.

Since that time, Amnesty International has expanded its focus and now explains that its vision is 'of a world in which every person enjoys all of the human rights enshrined in the Universal Declaration of Human Rights and other human rights instruments.' The original campaigns, however, mobilized public

Deprivations of life and liberty

105

support for a membership-based movement focused on such forgotten prisoners. This is part of the story of the growth of concern for human rights during the Cold War.

Known sometimes as 'prisoners of conscience' or 'political prisoners', such detainees were, and still are, the subject of human rights campaigns and protests. Their detention has come to be associated with regimes that generally disregard basic freedoms. Such detainees are arrested for expressing political opinions or claiming democratic rights, and their trials are often sorely lacking in the basic elements of a fair trial: the presumption of innocence, access to a lawyer of one's choice, and the chance to challenge the evidence before an independent judge.

More recently controversy has centred on secret detention and rendition operations by the US Central Intelligence Agency (CIA) with the complicity of other states. Secret detention is specifically designed to keep individuals outside the justice system and deny them the human rights protections which have been designed over the last decades in order to prevent torture and arbitrary deprivation of liberty. Although some of the most graphic details remain secret, the European Court of Human Rights has already held two European States accountable for their participation in these arrangements see below and Box 30. The following is taken from the Judgment given by the European Court of Human Rights in the *Al Nashiri v Poland* (2014) case:

> The Court observes that secret detention of terrorist suspects was a fundamental feature of the CIA rendition programme. As can be seen from the CIA declassified documents, the rationale behind the programme was specifically to remove those persons from any legal protection against torture and enforced disappearance and to strip them of any safeguards afforded by both the US Constitution and international law against arbitrary detention, to mention only the right to be brought before a judge and be tried

within a reasonable time or the habeas corpus guarantees. To this end, the whole scheme had to operate outside the jurisdiction of the US courts and in conditions securing its absolute secrecy, which required setting up, in cooperation with the host countries, overseas detention facilities.

One of the dangers with focusing on political prisoners and the absence of legal protection for suspected terrorists, is that we lose sight for a while of the bigger picture with regard to those deprived of their liberty. There is currently a worldwide population of over ten million detainees. The criteria of 'unpopular', 'marginalized', and 'vulnerable' can also be applied to these millions

Box 30 European Court of Human Rights, *El-Masri v the former Yugoslav Republic of Macedonia*

The Court observes that on 23 January 2004 the applicant, handcuffed and blindfolded, was taken from the hotel and driven to Skopje Airport. Placed in a room, he was beaten severely by several disguised men dressed in black. He was stripped and sodomised with an object. He was placed in an adult nappy and dressed in a dark blue short-sleeved tracksuit. Shackled and hooded, and subjected to total sensory deprivation, the applicant was forcibly marched to a CIA aircraft (a Boeing 737 with the tail number N313P), which was surrounded by Macedonian security agents who formed a cordon around the plane. When on the plane, he was thrown to the floor, chained down and forcibly tranquillised. While in that position, the applicant was flown to Kabul (Afghanistan) via Baghdad (Iraq)....In the Court's view, such treatment amounted to torture in breach of Article 3 of the Convention. The respondent State must be considered directly responsible for the violation of the applicant's rights under this head, since its agents actively facilitated the treatment and then failed to take any measures that might have been necessary in the circumstances of the case to prevent it from occurring.

of individuals incarcerated around the world. A huge number of these prisoners are subjected to conditions that fall far short of human rights standards. According to Penal Reform International

> In most prison systems, prisoners do not have the minimum space requirements recommended by international standards, spending up to 23 hours of the day, if not all day, in overcrowded cells. Overcrowding can be so severe that prisoners sleep in shifts, on top of each other, share beds or tie themselves to window bars so that they can sleep while standing.

In ending this discussion of detention, we should mention that an individual's freedom is not extinguished on arrest or conviction, the freedom is restricted to the extent that this is necessary; and the detaining authority is actually required to re-evaluate the necessity of all detention. As part of this freedom a detainee is entitled to demand that the authorities present a judge with an explanation of the legal basis for detention. This principle is sometimes known by the Latin expression *habeas corpus* after the historical judicial remedy, which, in the name of the Sovereign, forced anyone detaining another human being for any reason to produce the person before the judge and explain the legal justification for depriving that person of their liberty. The ancient remedy is now reflected in international law. The *International Covenant on Civil and Political Rights* in Article 9(4) states:

> Anyone who is deprived of his liberty by arrest or detention shall be entitled to take proceedings before a court, in order that that court may decide without delay on the lawfulness of his detention and order his release if the detention is not lawful.

The UN Human Rights Committee's General Comment 35 on liberty and security of the person (2014) explains:

The right [in Article 9(4)] applies to all detention by official action or pursuant to official authorization, including detention in connection with criminal proceedings, military detention, security detention, counter-terrorism detention, involuntary hospitalization, immigration detention, detention for extradition, and wholly groundless arrests. It also applies to detention for vagrancy or drug addiction, and detention for educational purposes of children in conflict with the law, and other forms of administrative detention. Detention within the meaning of paragraph 4 also includes house arrest and solitary confinement.

Chapter 6
Balancing rights—free speech and privacy

So far we have resisted the temptation to claim that human rights are about balancing individual freedoms and the collective interests of the community. Such claims are inappropriate when discussing torture, the right to life, the rights of detainees, and fair trial. Even if the majority demand that their interest in living in peace and security should take priority, the whole idea of human rights is that individuals' lives must be treated with respect, even where the majority consider that harsher treatment is justified.

Let us leave killing, torture, rendition, and arbitrary deprivations of liberty and look now at the formula for determining when limitations may indeed be imposed on other sorts of rights. The human rights we will consider in the rest of this chapter have built-in limitations. The thrust of international human rights law for these rights is that limitations to rights must be justified by reference to pre-existing *accessible* laws that allow for *proportionate* action *necessary* to achieve a *legitimate aim* (such as national security, public order, or the rights of others).

Free speech

In thinking about proportionate limitations on human rights, we have to consider what weight we wish to give to the fundamental values that we are seeking to promote. The weight we give the right then determines whether or not the restrictions are acceptable. Here we can mention a special role that is sometimes claimed for freedom of speech. The importance that is granted to protecting even offensive words, is explained by our sense that human progress comes when ideas can be challenged and authority can be questioned. While one may need to restrict speech that incites violence or represents harassment; the problem comes when this principle starts to stifle debate and critical inquiry. The value attached to freedom of expression can vary in different contexts, with many privileging this freedom due to its instrumental value for democracy and debate in all spheres of life. The explanation of the special value placed on freedom of expression was captured by the late Najib Mahfous, the Egyptian novelist and Nobel laureate. Writing in 1989 in the context of the threat to kill fellow novelist Salman Rushdie, he stated: 'As regards freedom of expression, I have said that it must be considered sacred and that thought can only be corrected by counter-thought.'

The prosecution of hate speech can of course be defended on the grounds that such action is designed to protect the human rights of religious minorities or defend equality. But this reasoning does not eliminate the lurking prospect of such prosecutions stifling critical voices and informed debate (see Box 31).

The Internet now presents us with new challenges. First, it creates new opportunities for harassment and unbearable cruelty towards some more vulnerable victims. The tragic consequences of such bullying have meant that national authorities have been forced to find ways to protect children and adults from the trauma of being ridiculed, harassed, or stalked on the Internet. Criminal prosecution may or may not be disproportionate. One set of guidelines from the UK explains that:

> Context is important and prosecutors should have regard to the fact
> that the context in which interactive social media dialogue takes

Box 31 'Should hate speech be a crime?', Peter Tatchell

Several Christian and Muslim street preachers have been arrested in Britain for hate speech. Their crime? They said that homosexuality is immoral and that gay people will go to hell. I disagree with them but opposed their prosecution. What they were saying was hurtful but not hateful. They did not express their views in a bullying or menacing tone.

Free speech is one of the hallmarks of a democratic society. It should only be restricted in extreme, compelling circumstances. Criminalizing views that are objectionable and offensive is the slippery slope to censorship and to the closing down of open debate. It is also counter-productive. It risks making martyrs of people with bigoted opinions and deflects from the real solution to hate speech: education and rational debate. Hate speech should be protested and challenged, not criminalized....

I was arrested for saying the homophobia and sexism of Islamist extremists is akin to the mentality of the Nazis. Separately, a youth was arrested for calling Scientology a dangerous cult. In both instances, it was deemed we had committed religious hate crimes.

place is quite different to the context in which other communications take place. Access is ubiquitous and instantaneous. Banter, jokes and offensive comments are commonplace and often spontaneous. Communications intended for a few may reach millions.

Similarly, Facebook, Twitter, and other social media have forced a re-evaluation of what it means to be a publisher, and what expectations employers can have when employees express themselves publicly on their 'private accounts'. Context will be essential to any determination and the concept that helps to determine when a restriction on freedom becomes a violation of human rights is *proportionality*.

Secondly, new technologies have allowed governments and others to gather much more information about us. Some of this information is essential for tackling ordinary crime and extraordinary threats from terrorism, but recent revelations about how this data is gathered has led to intensive debates about the need for the protection of privacy as a human right. In a report to the UN General Assembly, entitled 'Report on Human Rights and Counterterrorism', the UN's Special Rapporteur, Ben Emmerson QC, stated:

> The interception of communications provides a valuable source of information by which States can investigate, forestall and prosecute acts of terrorism and other serious crime. Most States now have the capacity to intercept and monitor calls made on a landline or mobile telephone, enabling an individual's location to be determined, his or her movements to be tracked through cell site analysis and his or her text messages to be read and recorded. Targeted surveillance also enables intelligence and law enforcement agencies to monitor the online activity of particular individuals, to penetrate databases and cloud facilities, and to capture the information stored on them. An increasing number of States are making use of malware systems that can be used to infiltrate an individual's computer or smartphone, to override its settings and to monitor its activity. . . .

> States' obligations under article 17 of the International Covenant on Civil and Political Rights include the obligation to respect the privacy and security of digital communications. This implies in principle that individuals have the right to share information and ideas with one another without interference by the State, secure in the knowledge that their communication will reach and be read by the intended recipients alone. Measures that interfere with this right must be authorized by domestic law that is accessible and

precise and that conforms with the requirements of the Covenant. They must also pursue a legitimate aim and meet the tests of necessity and proportionality.

Privacy

Thinking about the notion of privacy forces us to confront fundamental issues at the heart of human rights. Although there is a popular perception that 'time-honoured' rights to privacy are now constantly under attack, it is not at all clear where the notion of privacy came from. If we trace the origin of the concept, we find that privacy is not a traditional constitutional right; one does not find 18th century revolutionary demands for privacy. In fact, the protection of privacy seems to have developed in an ad hoc way in response to feelings of outrage or embarrassment as the need arose. In human rights law, privacy has become a residual right, used to buttress claims that might otherwise be based on respect for dignity, home, correspondence, sexuality, identity, or family.

Articulating the scope of this right is hard, not only do we have to take into account changing expectations and the government's increasing need to tackle crime and terrorism, but we also soon bump up against other people's human rights which also have to be respected. The right to privacy may extend only to the point where it does not unreasonably or disproportionately restrict someone else's right to freedom of expression or right to information. However, when we move away from the property-based notion of a right (where the right to privacy would protect, for example, images and personality), to modern notions of private and family life, we find it harder to delimit the right. This is, of course, the strength of the notion of privacy, in that it can adapt to meet changing expectations and technological advances involving data storage, telephone hacking, mass surveillance technology for emails, website visits and telephone calls, digital images, and DNA identification.

We might identify at least five contemporary dimensions to privacy. First, there is a desire to be free from observation. From this, rights may flow with regard to strip searches, detention, medical situations, hidden cameras, and other forms of surveillance. Second, there is a desire to restrict circulation of information and images about ourselves, especially where knowledge about such information could be embarrassing or prejudicial to our interests. Third, there is an interest in being able to communicate with others without third parties eavesdropping or monitoring our communications. Although the original protection in the human rights treaties covered 'correspondence', the scope of privacy protection has been extended to challenge telephone tapping, hacking, monitoring of the sorts of calls made, and employers' scrutiny of employees' emails. Fourth, our physical and mental well-being needs protection. The law of privacy has been developed to guarantee protection from domestic violence, sexual abuse, corporal punishment, and environmental hazards. Fifth, it is felt that space should be made so that we can develop our personalities free from control. If we are not free to make certain choices about sex, identity, and association then we may fail to develop our personalities to their full potential. In this way, international human rights treaties have been successfully used to challenge laws that criminalized consensual homosexual activity.

Privacy and the attempt to shield the private sphere from human rights protection

But the concept of privacy has another side. Privacy has been used to shield violence against women from interference by law enforcement officials. Privacy has also been invoked as a justification for racial discrimination when hiring domestic staff or excluding people from clubs and associations. The concept of a private sphere free from governmental interference has meant that issues of marital rape, child abuse, and female genital mutilation were not seen as part of the human rights debate, and that dealing with these issues meant invading someone's privacy.

These problems have been compounded by the notion of a public/private divide in law. Many legal systems have evolved around the idea that public law (including human rights protection) should regulate issues concerning governmental authorities, whilst private law regulates disputes between private entities that are not connected to the state or local authorities. By implication, it is sometimes said that activity in the private sphere is not the business of the public authorities. According to this line of argument, concerns relating to human dignity in this private sphere cannot therefore be remedied through state intervention or recourse to human rights law. Furthermore, to compound this exclusionary policy, international human rights law has been developed through the consideration of *states'* obligations under the various treaties they have agreed to. Because courts and committees can usually only hear complaints against the governments of these states, an assumption has arisen that all violations of human rights require the involvement of the government. In many quarters violations in the private sphere were simply not considered to be covered by international human rights law or something that should be considered a matter of human rights at all.

This has changed. First, the international bodies established under the human rights treaties have interpreted governments' obligations as giving rise to duties to protect individuals even from attacks on their rights by private individuals and other non-state entities. These obligations are often known as positive obligations, due diligence obligations, or obligations to protect. This evolution can be traced to a series of cases and reports in the 1980s and 1990s. Second, the development of international criminal law in the following decades has highlighted questions of individual responsibility for violations of international law. The fact is that some of the worst atrocities the international community has to deal with take place without any question of governmental involvement. Obvious examples include the rapes, torture, and civilian massacres carried out by rebel groups. There is now a good argument that such non-state actors have certain human rights obligations. Indeed, states held special sessions of the UN Human Rights Council in 2014 and 2015 and condemned in the strongest terms the systematic violations and abuses of human rights which result from the acts of the 'Islamic state' and the 'gross abuses of international human rights law' perpetrated by Boko Harem. In turn, the scope of human rights obligations is coming to be seen as having an impact on other non-state actors, such as the United Nations and NATO (in the context of their peace operations), international financial institutions (such as the World Bank and the International Monetary Fund), multinational corporations and other forms of businesses, and all sorts of political parties, religious groups, nursing homes, unions, clubs, and associations.

The traditional distinction between public and private, and the consequent exclusion of domestic and family matters from the public sphere, has led to a careful feminist critique of the construction of the public/private divide and its implications for women and women's rights. It has sometimes been suggested that abolishing the notion of a public/private divide is essential to ensure that oppression in the private sphere would be tackled as a matter of public political concern. The solution, however, is not to abolish the right to privacy (however problematic its past use): privacy claims are proving effective to ensure a degree of control over one's body, one's sexual relations, and over personal information and communication. The way forward is to take women's claims seriously and acknowledge that human rights apply in the private sphere.

Balancing privacy and other values

Balancing the right to privacy with the competing right to freedom of expression is certainly contextual, one might even say cultural. Human rights simultaneously claim to protect freedom of expression and the right to privacy. How to choose? Here we have to admit that the human rights framework is not akin to a set of traffic regulations or simple road rules. There is plenty of room for different people, different judges even, to come to different conclusions, and again everything depends on context. But at least in the context of the cases coming before the European Court of Human Rights an attempt has been made more recently to set out relevant criteria for determining whether a publication can be suppressed in order to protect someone's privacy. A recent case concerned a book by the former partner of the Finnish Prime Minister. While the Court has constantly stressed that the need for information about political figures is greater than that associated with individuals with no public role, the case turned on the published details of the couple's sex life. The Court applied its criteria and found that publication of this information could legitimately be sanctioned through criminal prosecution (see Box 32).

The expansion of the concept of privacy to protect people from pollution, including noise pollution, illustrates the point that privacy is not considered an absolute right and that decision makers have a complex task in determining whether an interference with the enjoyment of this right is justified. In 2001, residents near Heathrow Airport succeeded in convincing a Chamber of the European Court of Human Rights (by five votes to two) that the noise levels at night were an unjustifiable interference with their effective enjoyment of their right to respect for their homes and their private and family lives. The Grand Chamber, which deals with cases of exceptional importance, later held by twelve votes to five that the Government had struck the correct balance between the rights of the residents and the rights of others to travel and pursue competitive commercial operations (in turn considered necessary for the 'economic well-being' of the country). The dissenters disagreed and felt the balance had not been properly struck. As they put it:

> the close connection between human rights protection and the
> urgent need for a decontamination of the environment leads us to

Box 32 European Court of Human Rights, *Ruusunen v Finland*

The limits of permissible criticism are wider as regards a politician than as regards a private individual. Unlike the latter, the former inevitably and knowingly lay themselves open to close scrutiny of their words and deeds by journalists and the public at large, and they must consequently display a greater degree of tolerance.... Similar considerations apply also to persons in the public eye.... In certain circumstances, even where a person is known to the general public, he or she may rely on a 'legitimate expectation' of protection of and respect for his or her private life.... The Court went on to identify a number of criteria as being relevant where the right of freedom of expression is being balanced against the right to respect for private life.... namely

(i)   contribution to a debate of general interest;
(ii) how well-known is the person concerned and what is the subject of the report;
(iii) prior conduct of the person concerned;
(iv) method of obtaining the information and its veracity/ circumstances in which the photographs were taken;
(v)   content, form and consequences of the publication; and
(vi) severity of the sanction imposed.

perceive health as the most basic human need and as pre-eminent. After all, as in this case, what do human rights pertaining to the privacy of the home mean if, day and night, constantly or intermittently, it reverberates with the roar of aircraft engines?

Let us now briefly try to understand the emerging 'right to be forgotten' as an aspect of the right to privacy. The prospect of always being associated with a particular story or image that has been posted on the Internet can obviously be distressing. But if the events depicted are true, what about the Internet user's competing right to information? Or the publisher's right to freedom of expression? The so-called '*Google Spain Case*' concerned a man who wished to have a newspaper story about him removed from Internet search results. The story was about an auction for the recovery of social security debts. The concern is that today, by typing a name into a search engine one can find out so much interrelated information about someone that the total picture can amount to an invasion of privacy. The Court of Justice of the European Union upheld his rights to protection of personal data and private life, stating that in each case the search engine (in this case Google) would have to consider the sensitivity for the individual of the data which is presented in the search, and weigh this against the public interest in access to that information. Although the Court gave greater weight to the right to privacy over the rights of Internet users in this case, they added that the interest of the public in having the information may vary 'according to the role played by the data subject in public life'. In the first four months after the ruling Google received 135,000 requests referring to 470,000 links.

Proportionality

We have looked at limitations on privacy and freedom of expression to illustrate how rights may be limited and competing values balanced. Similar tensions exist when one comes to examine freedom of assembly, association, or the right to manifest one's religion. We will return to issues of religion in Chapter 8, for the moment let us simply summarize how limitations on human rights are applied in practice. The key is to understand what is often referred to in broad terms as a proportionality test. The concept of proportionality is common to determining the limitations on any human right that can be restricted. These rights can be restricted to the extent that the limit placed on them is proportionate to the aim pursued. A decision maker is obliged to adopt a four-stage process to determine whether the interference with a human right represents a legitimate limitation on the right concerned. This can be summarized as follows:

- Is there a legitimate aim to the interference?
- Is the interference prescribed by a clear and accessible law?
- Is the interference proportionate to the identified legitimate aim and necessary in a democratic society?
- Is there protection against arbitrary exercise of this interference?

The human rights approach therefore provides us with more than a slogan. It demands that a government that interferes with individual freedoms can point to a legitimate aim that justifies its actions, that the justification be in accordance with laws that are precise and accessible to the individual, and that the interference is proportionate and necessary in the circumstances.

Chapter 7
Food, education, health, housing, and work

'Human rights begin with breakfast': this quip from the former President of Senegal, Léopold Senghor, prompts many to react in alarm. Some see this assertion as part of an argument that certain rights, such as the right to food, need to be properly secured before one can turn to the luxury of the right to vote or to the privilege of freedom of expression. Indeed, many subscribe to a so-called 'full belly thesis', according to which subsistence rights to food and water have to be secured before turning to civil and political rights relating to political participation, arbitrary detention, freedom of expression, or privacy. Such argumentation is not as prevalent as it used to be (at least in government circles). Today all governments accept (most of the time) that there should be no prioritization among different types of rights. Different types of rights are seen to be mutually reinforcing: better nutrition, health, and education will lead to improvements in political freedoms and the rule of law; similarly, freedom of expression and association can ensure that the best decisions are taken to protect rights to food, health, and work. Despite the logic of such a desire to secure 'all rights for all people', traditional assumptions about what constitute 'proper' human rights still persist. One does not have to look very far to find commentators and others urging human rights organizations to resist being distracted by economic and social rights, which they would further say are not rights at all (see Box 33).

Box 33 *The Economist*, 'Stand up for your rights: the old stuffy ones, that is: newer ones are distractions', 24 March 2007

Rights being good things, you might suppose that the more of them you campaign for the better. Why not add pressing social and economic concerns to stuffy old political rights such as free speech, free elections and due process of law? What use is a vote if you are starving? Are not access to jobs, housing, health care and food basic rights too? No: few rights are truly universal, and letting them multiply weakens them.

Food, jobs and housing are certainly necessities. But no useful purpose is served by calling them 'rights'. When a government locks someone up without a fair trial, the victim, perpetrator and remedy are pretty clear. This clarity seldom applies to social and economic 'rights'. It is hard enough to determine whether such a right has been infringed, let alone who should provide a remedy, or how. Who should be educated in which subjects for how long at what cost in taxpayers' money is a political question best settled at the ballot box. So is how much to spend on what kind of health care. And no economic system known to man guarantees a proper job for everyone all the time: even the Soviet Union's much-boasted full employment was based on the principle 'they pretend to pay us and we pretend to work'.

Such an approach probably conceals a sense that such rights get in the way of rational choice and economic efficiency. Alternatively, those who wish to confine human rights to issues such as free speech and fair trial may have simply underestimated how much we now care about poverty and disease, not only when it affects us—but also when it affects other people. In any event, for a political philosopher like Charles Beitz, it makes no sense to define human rights as dependent on traditional historical natural rights theories. The international practice related to human rights is a fact, and that practice includes efforts to ensure economic and social rights (see Box 34).

The traditional narrow reading of human rights is, today, rarely explicitly defended in international relations. The expression 'human rights' covers not only civil and political rights such as freedom from torture, slavery, and arbitrary detention, but also economic, social, and cultural rights. In the words of the 1948 Universal Declaration:

> Everyone has the right to a standard of living adequate for the health and well-being of himself and of his family, including food, clothing, housing and medical care and necessary social services, and the right to security in the event of unemployment, sickness, disability, widowhood, old age or other lack of livelihood in circumstances beyond his control.

Box 34 C. R. Beitz, *The Idea of Human Rights*

Human rights are sometimes described as timeless—as protections that might reasonably be demanded in all times and places. But this description is difficult to reconcile with the content of international doctrine. Many of the threats protected against (e.g. unfair pay, lack of educational opportunity and access to medical care, loss of nationality) arise distinctively in modern or modernizing societies; they are not generic in the way that assault, say, was conceived as a threat in traditional 'state of nature' theories. Moreover, some human rights are only comprehensible against a background assumption that certain types of institutions either do or can be brought to exist—for example, the rule of law, elections for public office, a public capacity for taxation and welfare provision, at least a rudimentary administrative state. Modern human rights doctrine cannot plausibly be regarded as seeking to articulate protections of timeless significance; it speaks to what might be described broadly as the conditions of modern life.

International disagreement now concerns, first, the appropriate mechanisms for the enforcement of such rights, and second, the exact scope of these rights. Before turning to the interpretation of the scope of these rights, let us consider the perceived problem of enforcement.

A main concern is that economic and social policy is best determined by policy makers who are democratically accountable, and not by unelected judges with no specialized knowledge of how to prioritize the distribution of limited resources (see Box 35). In a context such as health, it is clear that health authorities and hospitals may have to deny some people treatment when this represents an unreasonable strain on limited resources. Those who support increasing the judicial enforcement of economic, social, and cultural rights point out that protecting civil and political rights also involves deciding questions with resource implications: the provision of humane conditions for detainees has resource implications; establishing the pre-conditions for

Box 35 C. Gearty, 'Against judicial enforcement'

Courts are not suitable places to receive, much less assess, the kind of empirical data and guesses about future trends that should underpin all social policy (including the provision of social rights). This is more than a reservation based on lack of equipment for the job . . . ; it is primarily an observation on the incompetence of the judicial forum however seemingly well-provided for the decision it may appear to be. The point is that it is not the right site to decide these things and the more you fiddle with its procedures to make it the right place (special briefs on socio-economic data and the like; advice from NGOs; expert evidence on the wider social impact of a proposed ruling; and so on), the more any such tribunal looks increasingly like an executive officer, but without the usual democratic necessities of electoral legitimacy and public accountability.

truly free and fair elections likewise costs money. But there remains a tension regarding the appropriateness of economic and social rights for judicial enforcement. The result is that, in those instances when courts have adjudicated economic, social, and cultural rights, judges have been careful not to impinge overly on the roles of the legislature and executive. For example, the judiciary in South Africa has reminded the government of its duty to justify restrictions on access to health care, and demanded that the government develops policies to ensure housing for the most marginalized. As with civil and political rights, the judiciary may remind governments that they have duties to ensure that legislation is introduced to ensure that rights can be enjoyed and protected under an effective legal system. Let us now look at some economic and social rights in a little more detail.

Food

The existence of the right to food does not mean that the government has to provide free food for all. The right to food is shorthand for a more complex set of obligations relating to 'food security' which involves ensuring access to food, and planning for shortages and distribution problems. We can start with the immediate obligations. First, the government should avoid undermining food security and should plan for the needs of the population. In particular, there should be no violation of the right to food through the unjustified destruction of crops or evictions from land. Furthermore, there must be no discrimination with regard to access to food. These immediate obligations can be seen as part of a duty to *respect* the right to food.

A second level of obligation concerns the duty to *protect* the right to food. Here we find obligations to protect individuals from interference with their right to food from other actors. So, for example, the state may have a duty to regulate with regard to food safety. In some contexts, this may require the state to guarantee that title to land is ensured to those who have a close cultural link to the land—such as indigenous peoples.

The third level is variously expressed as an obligation to *fulfil, assist, facilitate, or provide*. This means, on the one hand, strengthening access to food by ensuring that people have the resources for food security through stimulating employment, engaging in land reform, and developing transport and storage facilities. On the other hand, the state may have to provide food or social security to fulfil basic needs in the situations referred to in the Universal Declaration (cited earlier in this chapter) in which the individual is subject to 'unemployment, sickness, disability, widowhood, old age or other lack of livelihood in circumstances beyond his control'.

In recent years, considerable focus has been placed on the 'right to water' as water has come to be regarded as a part of a globalized services market. Often subsumed under the right to food, the right to water is increasingly raised in the context of privatization of public utilities, and in particular with regard to multinational companies which have been accused of pricing parts of the population out of the market, resulting in a denial of the right to water.

Education

The right to education is crucial to empowering people to be able to enjoy their other rights. The right to education involves not only obligations to refrain from interfering with the right by closing schools, or discriminating against certain pupils, but also includes obligations to fulfil the right to education by providing compulsory, free primary education for all. The right to education has been developed at the doctrinal level to encompass what is known as a '4As' approach: availability, accessibility, acceptability, and adaptability. (Some might hear echoes here of the 3Rs—reading, writing, and arithmetic.)

First, education has to be *available* in a functional sense so that, in the words of the UN Committee on Economic Social and Cultural Rights, there has to be: 'protection from the elements, sanitation facilities for both sexes, safe drinking water, trained teachers receiving domestically competitive salaries, [and] teaching materials.' The late UN expert Katerina Tomaševski pointed out that for availability to be meaningful, rather than formal, schools have actually to attract children. Not only must schools be formally open to both boys and girls, but they should be monitored to ensure that girls and boys are retained in school. Inadequate teaching or lack of relevant schoolbooks will mean that children and parents will see little point in using the available facilities, and the government will fail in its obligation to provide compulsory primary education that is available free to all.

Second, the state must ensure that schools and programmes are *accessible* to all. This has three dimensions. First, accessibility means *non-discrimination*. This is an obligation on states with immediate effect. Affirmative action, or 'temporary special measures', intended to bring about equality for men and women, or for disadvantaged groups, is not considered a violation of the non-discrimination rule as long as it does not continue unnecessarily. Discrimination against girls remains a real problem. For example, pregnancy can trigger girls being expelled from school in violation of their right to education. Furthermore, for some parents, it is seen as economically irrational to invest in their daughters' education; they therefore privilege their boys' education. The second dimension to accessibility is *physical accessibility*. This means that children with disabilities are not excluded due to the design of the buildings, and that education is within physical reach geographically. The third dimension is *economic accessibility*. While international law demands that education be free in the elementary and fundamental stages, there is a weaker obligation with regard to secondary education so that there should be a progression towards free secondary education. This means that, although priority is to be given to ensuring free primary education, governments must also take concrete steps to ensure free secondary and tertiary education.

Acceptability is the concept used to describe the importance of ensuring that education is conducted in a way that is acceptable to children and parents. An acceptable environment is about not only material conditions and the absence of violence, but also about enabling children to develop and learn. Corporal punishment in schools is a violation of the rights of the child, and bullying can be addressed in terms of human rights language which refers to cruel, inhuman, and degrading treatment.

The fourth aspect of the right to education, the concept of *adaptability*, raises fundamental questions about education. What is education for? And who decides? As long as education is geared solely to admission to the next (sometimes selective) stage of education, some children will be ill-equipped for life.

Health

The right to health does not mean that we have the right to be healthy. The right to health is defined by UN expert Paul Hunt as:

> a right to an effective and integrated health system, encompassing health care and the underlying determinants of health, which is responsive to national and local priorities, and accessible to all.

He uses the *accessibility* prism to point out that the right to health means that health care:

> must be accessible to all, not just the wealthy, but also those living in poverty; not just majority ethnic groups, but minorities and indigenous peoples, too; not just those living in urban areas, but also remote villagers; not just men, but also women. The health system has to be accessible to all disadvantaged individuals and communities.

The UN Committee on Economic, Social and Cultural Rights has developed an interpretation of the right to health that uses the same triptych of obligations to respect, protect, and fulfil that we discussed earlier for the right to food.

First, the obligation to *respect* requires states to avoid measures that could prevent the enjoyment of the right. Therefore, states are under the obligation to *respect* the right to health by, *inter alia*, refraining from (i) denying or limiting equal access for all persons to preventive, curative, and palliative health services; (ii) prohibiting or impeding traditional preventive care, healing practices, and medicines; (iii) marketing unsafe drugs; (iv) applying coercive medical treatments; (v) limiting access to contraceptives and other means of maintaining sexual and reproductive health; and (vi) censoring, withholding, or intentionally misrepresenting health-related information, including sexual education and information, as well as preventing people's participation in health-related matters.

Second, the obligation to *protect* requires states to take measures that prevent third parties from interfering with the right to adequate health care. Obligations to *protect* include, therefore, the duties of states to (i) adopt legislation or to take other measures ensuring equal access to health care and health-related services provided by third parties; (ii) ensure that privatization of the health sector does not constitute a threat to the availability, accessibility, acceptability, and quality of health facilities, goods, and services; (iii) control the marketing of medical equipment and medicines by third parties; (iv) prevent third parties from coercing women to undergo traditional practices, such as female genital mutilation; and (v) take measures to protect all vulnerable or marginalized groups of society, in particular women, children, adolescents, and older persons.

Finally, the obligation to *fulfil* requires states to take positive measures that enable individuals and groups to enjoy the right to health. The obligation to *fulfil* requires states, for instance, to (i) give sufficient recognition to the right to health in the national, political, and legal systems, preferably by way of legislative implementation; (ii) adopt a national health policy with a detailed plan for realizing the right to health; (iii) ensure provision of health care, including immunization programmes against the major infectious diseases; (iv) ensure equal access for all to the underlying determinants of health, such as nutritiously safe food and potable drinking water, basic sanitation, and adequate housing and living conditions; (v) ensure the appropriate training of doctors and other medical personnel, the provision of sufficient numbers of hospitals, clinics, and other health-related facilities with due regard to equitable distribution throughout the country; (vi) provide a public, private, or mixed health insurance system that is affordable for all; (vii) promote medical research and health education; and (viii) promote information campaigns, in particular with respect to HIV/AIDS, sexual and reproductive health, traditional practices, domestic violence, the abuse of alcohol, and the use of cigarettes, drugs, and other harmful substances.

This all looks perfect on paper, and left to their own devices, most governments would claim they are doing their best to progressively realize all of these goals, taking into account their available resources. Hunt and others have therefore started to develop an accountability schema using indicators and benchmarks. This is how it works. First, key indicators are chosen. For example an indicator could be the proportion of births attended by skilled health personnel. These should be disaggregated for race, or other relevant characteristics, as appropriate. The challenge is to ensure that all agencies and human rights bodies concentrate on equivalent indicators. The second step is for the government to set national benchmarks as a time-bound target. The government would propose various national benchmarks. The relevant treaty monitoring body should approve or adjust the benchmark to ensure that the state fulfils its international obligations in this context. Lastly, as part of any periodic review, these benchmarks are reviewed by the various international and national actors concerned and, in this way, progress or regression can be monitored and, if necessary, corrected. Here we are not really in the presence of judicially enforceable remedies for violations of rights; we are in the realm of thinking about issues such as health or trade or development in terms of a rights-based approach which focuses on concepts such as participation, accountability, non-discrimination, empowerment, and links to international legal norms.

A contemporary controversy in the context of the right to health is the perceived clash with the intellectual property rights of multinational pharmaceutical companies. While states may have a duty under some legal regimes to protect intellectual property rights in ways that ensure the welfare of the society, intellectual property rights are not absolute human rights like the right not to be tortured. The interests of companies in earning enough from sales of their pharmaceuticals to enable them to fund further research and development have to be weighed by the state against the human rights of those needing access to health care. So far, this issue has remained a question of political action rather than a judicial weighing of competing rights.

Housing

We have just seen that the right to health does not mean that an individual can demand unlimited resources from the government. Similarly, Scott Leckie, in one of his core contributions to the topic, starts out by assuring the reader that, 'The legal texts establishing housing rights norms obviously were not created to ensure the right of everyone to inhabit a luxurious mansion, surrounded by well sculpted gardens.' It is the concept of *adequacy* that has been central to the development of the right to housing since its inclusion in the Universal Declaration of Human Rights in 1948. This concept takes us beyond a minimal notion of shelter, the roof over one's head, and focuses our attention on the crucial concerns of the individual holders of the right. Again commentators use the respect, protect, fulfil, provide framework to flesh out the obligations on a state. Indeed, according to Asbjørn Eide:

> States have, first, a duty to respect the housing found by people themselves by abstaining from forcible evictions and displacements. Second, they must protect the tenure of existing housing against interference or unjustified evictions by third parties and adopt and enforce the necessary regulations to ensure necessary quality of housing. Third, they have an obligation through regulatory functions to facilitate the opportunity of everyone to find affordable housing. Fourth, in exceptional circumstances and in regard to particularly vulnerable groups, they have to provide necessary housing when individuals or groups cannot manage to do so themselves.

Perhaps the greatest focus in this area has been on the legal and procedural protections that have to be developed in the context of 'forced evictions' as defined in human rights law. The general prohibition on forced evictions is an obligation of immediate effect. This immediate obligation is now at the heart of housing rights activism. Part of the focus has been on large-scale development projects. In turn, this has prompted the adoption of guidelines on involuntary resettlement by the Organization for Economic Cooperation and Development, as well as by the World Bank.

These elaborate guidelines, norms, and recommendations have, in some cases, been used to prevent or halt forced evictions and remind governments that housing is a human rights issue. But things are not really so simple. As with other rights, such as the right to privacy, housing rights come up against other fundamental rights claims. Consider the right to water of the people of Gujarat; and the rights of those about to be displaced from their housing in the area designated to be flooded in order to complete the Narmada Dam project in India. Invoking human rights does not determine the dilemma. Human rights principles, however, provide the vocabulary for the evaluation of the decision making process. The majority of the Indian Supreme Court was careful to avoid replacing the government's decisions with a judicial preference for one set of rights claims.

> Conflicting rights had to be considered. If for one set of people namely those of Gujarat, there was only one solution, namely, construction of a dam, the same would have an adverse effect on another set of people whose houses and agricultural land would be submerged in water....When a decision is taken by the Government after due consideration and full application of mind, the Court is not to sit in appeal over such decision.

At the international level, however, human rights courts may sometimes feel they have to step in to halt threats to communities and may be less concerned about interfering with democratic decision making. In 2013, in one of its first decisions, the African Court of Human and Peoples' Rights ordered Kenya to reinstate restrictions related to land transactions in order to protect the rights of the 15,000 members of the Ogiek Community who inhabit the Mau Forest.

In closing this section on housing, we should point out that some actions against the right to housing amount to international crimes and now give rise to individual criminal responsibility. Starting with the crimes mentioned in the Rome Statute for the International Criminal Court, we could mention that a widespread or systematic attack against the civilian population involving the deportation or forced transfer of persons constitutes an international crime against humanity. Of direct relevance are war crimes involving the destruction of housing. The law here is complex and recognizes that there will be some necessary damage in times of armed conflict, but one might mention three separate international war crimes. First, the war crime of extensive destruction and appropriation of property by an Occupying Power, not justified by military necessity, and carried out unlawfully and wantonly; second, in an international armed conflict, the war crime of intentionally launching an attack in the knowledge that such attack will cause incidental loss of life or injury to civilians or damage to civilian objects which would be clearly excessive in relation to the concrete and direct overall military advantage anticipated; and, third, in the context of civil wars, destroying or seizing the property of an adversary unless such destruction or seizure is imperatively demanded by the necessities of the conflict.

Those who order, facilitate, or carry out such destruction of housing commit war crimes and could be prosecuted, not just in a relevant international criminal tribunal, but in the courts of any state willing to bring such suspected war criminals to justice.

Work

Various national and local struggles for workers' rights have encompassed the fight against slavery and forced labour, claims for decent working conditions and fair wages, the right to form and join trade unions, and the right to strike. In some ways, these movements antedate the modern human rights movement. International standards and procedures were elaborated through the work of the International Labour Organization (ILO), established in 1919 at the end of the First World War, and against the background of the Russian Revolution. At that time, an international focus was regarded as crucial to counterbalance the increasing appeal of an advancing Communism promising to vindicate workers' rights. Social justice was seen in the context of both world wars as essential to achieve lasting peace. The ILO went on to develop detailed Conventions and elaborate mechanisms for monitoring compliance with the various standards.

A new era began in 1998 as a result of a divisive discussion about protecting workers' rights through the World Trade Organization's international trade law regime. There was considerable unease that introducing labour rights issues through a social clause into the trade regime would allow richer states to exclude imports from developing countries on the grounds that workers in those countries were neither properly paid nor afforded the sorts of labour rights they would enjoy in the developed world. Developing countries would thereby be precluded from enjoying the economic benefits of their comparative advantage in cheap labour. It was decided that the issue of workers' rights should be shunted out of the trade arena and left to the ILO. The ILO responded by taking a fresh look at international labour rights. The rights were then streamlined and repackaged in the ILO Declaration on Fundamental Principles and Rights at Work. The resulting principles were said to be: freedom of association and the effective recognition of the right to collective bargaining; the elimination of all forms of forced or compulsory labour; the effective abolition of child labour; and the elimination of discrimination in respect of employment and occupation.

An increasing awareness that a state-centric approach to these issues failed to capture the activities of large corporations in a globalized market-place has led to multiple initiatives to make corporations more responsible. Codes of conduct, ethical investment schemes, 'national contact points' within states associated with the Organisation for Economic Co-operation and Development, and ambitious lawsuits all seek to focus on the abuses committed by corporations. In 2005 the United Nations appointed John Ruggie to identify and clarify the relevant human rights standards for corporate responsibility and accountability. In 2011 the resulting Guiding Principles were endorsed by the Human Rights Council and rest on a protect, respect, remedy framework with three pillars:

- the state duty to protect against human rights abuses by third parties, including business enterprises, through appropriate policies, regulation, and adjudication;

- an independent corporate responsibility to respect human rights, which means that business enterprises should act with due diligence to avoid infringing on the rights of others and address adverse impacts with which they are involved;
- the need for greater access by victims to effective remedy, both judicial and non-judicial.

In Ruggie's words 'Simply, put: states must protect; companies must respect; and those who are harmed must have redress.'

A key principle clarifies that corporations have responsibilities to respect a wide range of rights. This is significant, as, for many years, corporations would often respond 'Human rights? They're none of our business!' Nevertheless, even if we have greater clarity for the normative framework, effective remedies are few and far between. There is a serious lack of accountability in the face of companies' failure to respect human rights as required by pillar two and paragraph 12 of the UN Guiding Principles on Business and Human Rights which states:

> 12. The responsibility of business enterprises to respect human rights refers to internationally recognized human rights—understood, at a minimum, as those expressed in the International Bill of Human Rights and the principles concerning fundamental rights set out in the International Labour Organization's Declaration on Fundamental Principles and Rights at Work.

The Covenant on Economic Social and Cultural Rights contains a right to work. The UN Committee on Economic, Social and Cultural Rights has, however, warned: 'The right to work should not be understood as an absolute and unconditional right to obtain employment.' Like some of the other rights we have been considering in this chapter, the idea evoked by the right to work does not in fact give rise to an obvious immediate entitlement. The package of component rights is complicated. The first is the right not to be subjected to forced labour. A second right demands that there should be access to the employment market. Third, there should be safe working conditions and just remuneration. Fourth, the right to form trade unions must be recognized; and, fifth, workers have the right not to be discriminated against, and to be protected from unfair dismissal. Finally, everyone has the right to social security in the event of unemployment.

Of course, some of the limitations we encountered in previous chapters will apply. States may be able to introduce certain restrictions on access to the labour market by foreigners (migrant workers); although once granted employment, there can usually be no excuse for discrimination against foreigners.

Human rights have not always been regarded as supportive of the aspirations of the trade union movement. Judges have considered the right to form trade unions to include a 'negative right of association' entitling workers to refuse to join a trade union. There have been attempts to present strike action or boycotts by trade union members as violations by the striking workers of a human right of employers to refuse to enter into agreements with trade unions.

While the principles of freedom of association at work and protection from unfair dismissal may be universally recognized, the detail of how these rights are implemented is dependent on ideology, political power, and cultural context. Some countries have a long tradition of recognizing the importance of giving trade unions a central role in negotiating working conditions; others see unions as a hindrance to flexibility and competitiveness. Such approaches are not fixed, and can change in response to social changes and the emergence of new majorities through the democratic process.

Regional integration, in contexts such as the European Union (EU), has driven a degree of harmonization of labour rights in order to ensure fair competition in the internal market. The economic logic of ensuring a level playing field in Europe has led, not only to concrete rules ensuring equal pay for men and women at work, but also to new protections related to harassment in the workplace. Furthermore, EU law has developed to demand prohibitions on racial and religious discrimination, as well as on discrimination in the workplace on the grounds of disability, age, and sexual orientation. We now turn to deal with discrimination in a little more detail.

Chapter 8
Discrimination and equality

As we have seen throughout this short book, discrimination is prohibited with regard to the enjoyment of all rights. We have discovered the immediate obligation to prevent discrimination, not only in the context of the enjoyment of civil and political rights (such as personal freedom from arbitrary detention, freedom of expression, political participation, and association), but also in the fields of food, water, health, education, housing, and work. Now we shall consider the prohibited grounds of discrimination, what new grounds may be emerging, and when drawing distinctions between people can be considered reasonable and therefore legitimate.

As we saw at the start of this book, for some, the foundation of human rights can be traced to the twin ideas that human beings are born equal in dignity and rights, and that all human beings have to be treated with equal concern and respect. Quite why we should treat others in this way, and exactly how far we should go to ensure that they are shown this respect remain tricky questions for moral philosophers. These discussions usually come close to admitting that there is something 'sacred' about each individual human being, and that, despite the existence of obvious inequalities at birth, justice and fairness demand that we design a system to give everyone equal access to opportunities and, in some versions, redistribute resources to ensure that the least well-off are prioritized in our attempts to achieve equality of outcomes. These philosophical approaches to human rights provide much of the ballast for the human rights rules on discrimination, and provide the moral case for developing these rules to achieve greater social justice on a global scale.

Another way to look at non-discrimination is through the lens of the campaigns and activists who built the human rights movement: anti-slavery, the fight for women's rights, anti-colonialism, anti-apartheid, anti-racism. Discrimination is also central to the concept of genocide and inherent in the concept of crimes against humanity. The injustice that stems from being treated adversely on account of one's gender, colour, or religion formed the human right to non-discrimination in its present form. The Universal Declaration of Human Rights proclaimed in 1948 that:

> Everyone is entitled to all the rights and freedoms set forth in this Declaration, without distinction of any kind, such as race, colour, sex, language, religion, political or other opinion, national or social origin, property, birth or other status.

The first thing to notice is that the ban on discrimination was limited to the enjoyment of the other rights in the Declaration. Since that time, international and national rules have extended the scope of non-discrimination obligations to most areas of life and to embrace conduct by private (or non-state) actors in addition to the government. Landlords, hotels, restaurants, employers, transportation companies, water and electricity providers, parks, swimming pools, and insurance schemes ought to be prohibited from discriminating on any of these grounds. The second thing to notice is that the list is not closed. Other grounds of discrimination may be prohibited. The UN Committees responsible for monitoring legal obligations under the Covenants of 1966 have extended the non-discrimination obligation to prohibit discrimination with regard to the rights in those treaties on grounds of sexual orientation, health status (including HIV or AIDS), physical or mental disability, age, and nationality. The third point to understand is that in some cases, drawing a distinction between people on a particular ground may be justified as reasonable, for example religious schools may restrict employment to followers of the relevant faith.

Reasonable differentiation and the issue of age

A case concerning age discrimination helps illustrate the idea of reasonable differentiation. An Australian airline pilot, Mr Love, complained to the UN Human Rights Committee that his compulsory retirement from Australian Airlines at the age of 60 constituted unlawful discrimination under the Covenant. First, the Committee determined that age could be considered as a prohibited ground of discrimination and considered that age was a prohibited 'status' even if not explicitly mentioned in the equality provisions of the Covenant. Second, it was noted that mandatory retirement ages may actually provide workers protection by limiting life-long working time. Third, the Human Rights Committee accepted that the distinction made on the basis of age pursued a legitimate aim: maximizing safety to passengers and others. This was neither arbitrary nor unreasonable. To paraphrase one of the members, Justice Bhagwati from the Indian Supreme Court: not every differentiation incurs the vice of discrimination.

Same-sex relationships and religion

Human rights reasoning also lies at the heart of new demands for equal rights in new areas such as same-sex marriage. Even before any developments could be discerned in international human rights law, the South African Constitutional Court found in favour of two women who wanted to get married to each other. At one level, the case turns on the application of the Constitution; at another level, the decision is a logical extension of the philosophy of human rights. Writing for the whole Court, Justice Albie Sachs explained:

A democratic, universalistic, caring and aspirationally egalitarian society embraces everyone and accepts people for who they are. To penalise people for being who and what they are is profoundly disrespectful of the human personality and violatory of equality. Equality means equal concern and respect across difference. It does not presuppose the elimination or suppression of difference. Respect for human rights requires the affirmation of self, not the denial of self.

But around the world, although there are now perhaps nearly forty countries which allow same-sex marriage or something nearly equivalent, there are, according to the Human Dignity Trust, seventy-nine jurisdictions which have laws which criminalize private, consensual sexual conduct between adults of the same sex (see Box 36). Often such legislation is justified on religious grounds. The tension between respecting religious beliefs and ensuring equality has been laid bare in a number of cases concerning individuals refusing on religious grounds to offer services to same sex couples or complaining that they were not entitled to wear religious symbols at work. Let us look at the context of four recent cases which were joined in a single judgment at the European Court of Human Rights. One case was brought by a Christian marriage registrar who had lost her job as a consequence of refusing to officiate over civil partnerships for same-sex couples; a second was brought by a relationship counsellor who refused to counsel homosexual couples. In both situations the Court felt that the employer (in the first, a public authority; in the second, a private corporation) was pursuing the justifiable aim of ensuring equality. The other two cases concerned a nurse who was prevented from wearing a cross on health and safety grounds; and a British Airways worker who had been similarly prevented from wearing a cross but in this last case the

> **Box 36 Human Dignity Trust website (2014), seventy-nine jurisdictions with laws criminalizing private, consensual sexual conduct between adults of the same sex**
>
> Afghanistan, Algeria, Angola, Antigua and Barbuda, Bangladesh, Barbados, Belize, Bhutan, Botswana, Brunei, Burundi, Cameroon, Comoros, Cook Islands (New Zealand Associate), Dominica, Egypt, Eritrea, Ethiopia, Gambia, Gaza (Occupied Palestinian Territory), Ghana, Grenada, Guinea, Guyana, India, Indonesia (South Sumatra and Aceh Province), Iran, Iraq (status unclear), Jamaica, Kenya, Kiribati, Kuwait, Lebanon, Liberia, Libya, Malawi, Malaysia, Maldives, Mauritania, Mauritius, Morocco, Mozambique, Myanmar (Burma), Namibia, Nauru, Nigeria, Oman, Pakistan, Papua New Guinea, Qatar, St Kitts & Nevis, St Lucia, Saint Vincent & the Grenadines, Samoa, Saudi Arabia, Senegal, Seychelles, Sierra Leone, Singapore, Solomon Islands, Somalia, South Sudan, Sri Lanka, Sudan, Swaziland, Syria, Tanzania, Togo, Tonga, Trinidad & Tobago, Tunisia, Turkmenistan, Tuvalu, Uganda, United Arab Emirates, Uzbekistan, Yemen, Zambia, Zimbabwe.

rationale was that the company wished to project a certain corporate image. The claim by the nurse failed, while the British Airways worker succeeded in her claim, the Court found that too much weight had been given to the justification related to corporate image. So determining when a differential measure is discriminatory remains a very contextual exercise.

In the United States, the Supreme Court refused in 2010 to find a violation of freedom of expression or association where a student organization, the Christian Legal Society, was excluded from receiving funding from a public sector university because the organization operated a policy of applying their rules so that individuals were excluded where they engaged in 'unrepentant homosexual conduct', or held religious convictions different from those in the organization's Statement of Faith. The Justices in the majority seemed to be convinced by the university's policy of bringing together individuals with diverse backgrounds and beliefs, which in turn could encourage tolerance, cooperation, and learning among students. In the words of Justice Kennedy, 'A vibrant dialogue is not possible if students wall themselves off from opposing points of view.'

Courts in different countries have also been faced with a series of complaints by lesbian and gay couples where they have been refused hotel rooms or other arrangements on religious grounds. One technique has been to consider whether those refusing their services made 'reasonable accommodation'. We will also encounter this concept later in the section on discrimination on the basis of disability. The idea is that one considers whether reasonable steps had been taken to accommodate the rights of those being excluded, and is explained in a similar case by Lady Hale, the Vice President of the UK Supreme Court.

> In *Smith and Chymyshyn v Knights of Columbus and others* ... a lesbian couple had hired a hall owned by the Roman Catholic Church and let out on its behalf by the Knights in order to hold a reception after their marriage. The hall was available for public hire and they did not know of its connections with the Church. The letting was cancelled when the Knights learned of their purpose. The Tribunal accepted that the Knights could not be compelled to act in a manner contrary to their core belief that same sex marriages were wrong, but they had nevertheless failed in their duty of reasonable accommodation. They did not consider the effect their actions would have on the couple, did not think of meeting them to explain the situation and apologize, or offer to reimburse them for any expenses they had incurred or to help find another solution. In effect, they did not appreciate the affront to the couple's human dignity and do their best to soften the blow.

Foreigners

A major equality issue concerns the restrictions that are permitted with regard to non-nationals. At one level, discrimination against non-nationals is a form of racism or xenophobia which is offensive and irrational. At another level, it is accepted that states should be able to control immigration, to limit who can vote and stand in elections, and to limit access to employment or aspects of health care or education. Nevertheless, human rights principles demand that any such distinctions are justified as proportionate to a legitimate aim. So a rule that precludes foreigners from obtaining employment with the secret services could be considered proportionate to the aims of ensuring national security. Rules that demand higher university fees from foreigners could be proportionate to the aim of ensuring access to education for the local tax-paying population. On the other hand, migrant workers are not only protected by a specialized Convention (in force for only a few states), but also through a number of international opinions and interpretative statements. The UN Committee on the Elimination of Racial Discrimination has stated that:

> while States parties may refuse to offer jobs to non-citizens without a work permit, all individuals are entitled to the enjoyment of labour and employment rights, including the freedom of assembly and association, once an employment relationship has been initiated until it is terminated.

The same Committee reminds these states to:

> Take effective measures to prevent and redress the serious problems commonly faced by non-citizen workers, in particular by non-citizen domestic workers, including debt bondage, passport retention, illegal confinement, rape and physical assault.

This brings us back to the phenomenon of human trafficking. Trafficking illustrates how the human rights framework is moving beyond a simple focus on equality to develop new protections. Trafficking exposes its victims to further abuses in the country of destination, including violations of the right not to be subjected to forced labour and the right to be protected from inhumane treatment. The treaty adopted in 2000 to 'Prevent, Suppress and Punish Trafficking in Persons' addresses traffickers who use deception or coercion in their recruitment, transportation, transfer, harbouring, or receipt of persons. Their purpose is exploitation, which is stated to include 'at a minimum, the exploitation of the prostitution of others or other forms of sexual exploitation, forced labour or services, slavery or practices similar to slavery, servitude or the removal of organs'. The treaty is clear that the consent of the victim is irrelevant. Rather than address the victims of trafficking, the treaty focuses on creating criminal jurisdiction over the traffickers. The fate of the trafficked women, however, is left to rather vague demands that the receiving country consider adopting measures to allow the women to remain. States remain ready to use the option of deportation of the trafficked women, thus discouraging these women from seeking protection, and in some cases exposing them to further risks in their country of origin. The promise of human rights for all men and women is largely failing the victims of trafficking. The principle of equality is proving to be rather empty when considered against the rule that allows for these non-nationals to be deported.

One problem with the human right not to be discriminated against is that it usually assumes that you are being discriminated against while trying to exercise one of your other rights. Migrant workers and the victims of trafficking do not possess a right to enter a country or to have access to the employment market. Furthermore, discrimination principles rely on the idea of a comparator. Human rights are violated when you are treated less favourably than someone else in a comparable position. What if there is no obvious comparator? Women who are discriminated against for being pregnant, or minorities whose culture risks extinction may find that discrimination principles are of little use. A further problem relates to affirmative action (also known as positive discrimination). Human rights principles do allow for positive discrimination in the context of racial and sex discrimination, but such measures clearly run the risk of being challenged as fresh forms of discrimination. The acceptability of any affirmative action programme will depend entirely on the context. Again, different societies will have different priorities with regard to achieving the representation of certain minorities or disadvantaged groups in various sectors of society.

Violence against women

Despite these fundamental difficulties with the concept of non-discrimination, the human rights framework and the notion of equality have been adapted to create campaigns to deal with violence against women (see Figure 13 and Box 37).

More recently there has been a high-level mobilization around tackling conflict-related sexual violence, with the UN Secretary-General naming parties responsible for patterns of rape and other forms of sexual violence in situations of armed conflict that are on the Security Council's agenda. But do such parties care? What is the point of naming and shaming the shameless? It may be counter-intuitive, but there actually is a good case that not only governments, but also most rebel groups do eventually crave legitimacy in order to retain support and some form of moral superiority (even as compared to other rebel groups or the government they are fighting). Away from the United Nations, civil society groups such as Geneva Call have succeeded in altering rebel behaviour by getting such groups to sign 'deeds of commitment' banning landmines, protecting children, and prohibiting sexual violence and gender discrimination.

13. Amnesty International's high-profile campaign, supported here by Patrick Stewart, encourages people to speak out against domestic violence as a human rights issue.

Box 37 Amnesty International, *It's in Our Hands: Stop Violence against Women*

One of the achievements of women's rights activists has been to demonstrate that violence against women is a human rights violation. This changes the perception of violence against women from a private matter to one of public concern and means that public authorities are required to take action. The parallel development of international and regional human rights standards reinforces this accountability. Framing violence against women as a human rights issue creates a common language for the work of anti-violence activists and facilitates global and regional networks....

One of the most powerful features of the human rights framework is the core principle that human rights are universal—all people have equal rights by virtue of being human. The appeal to universality counters one of the most common excuses used to justify violence against women, that it is acceptable because it is part of the society's culture. All human rights should be enjoyed by all people, and culture or tradition do not excuse the violation of women's basic human rights. Universality does not impose uniformity or deny diversity. Human rights can be universal only if understood in terms of the rich range of different cultures and experiences.

Persons with disabilities

The 2006 Convention on the Rights of Persons with Disabilities marked a turning point in the way disability was dealt with as a matter of international concern. As Quinn and Mahony explain, the default setting had been 'a mixture of charity, paternalism and social policy.' The shift to the human rights framework has forced new possibilities for ensuring not only non-discrimination, but also meaningful forms of equality. Quinn and Mahony again:

the human rights revolution in the context of disability has to do with making the human being behind the disability visible and extending the benefits of the 'rule of law' to all and not just to some or indeed to most. Most importantly, it has to do with treating persons with disabilities as 'subjects' with full legal personhood as distinct from 'objects' to be managed and cared for.

The Convention goes beyond non-discrimination and tackles the measures which are needed to ensure the human rights of persons with disability. In particular it moves beyond formal equality to substantive equality through the concept of 'reasonable accommodation', and moves away from any sort of 'best interests' approach, as one finds in children's rights, towards the incorporation of equal recognition before the law with 'supported decision making' (see Box 38).

Box 38 Convention on the Rights of Persons with Disabilities (excerpts. emphasis added)

States Parties shall prohibit all *discrimination on the basis of disability* and guarantee to persons with disabilities equal and effective legal protection against discrimination on all grounds.

'Discrimination on the basis of disability' means any distinction, exclusion or restriction on the basis of disability which has the purpose or effect of impairing or nullifying the recognition, enjoyment or exercise, on an equal basis with others, of all human rights and fundamental freedoms in the political, economic, social, cultural, civil or any other field. It includes all forms of discrimination, including denial of *reasonable accommodation*;

In order to promote equality and eliminate discrimination, States Parties shall take all appropriate steps to ensure that *reasonable accommodation* is provided.

Box 38 Continued

'*Reasonable accommodation*' means necessary and appropriate modification and adjustments not imposing a disproportionate or undue burden, where needed in a particular case, to ensure to persons with disabilities the enjoyment or exercise on an equal basis with others of all human rights and fundamental freedoms;

The principles of the present Convention shall be:

a. Respect for inherent dignity, individual autonomy including the freedom to make one's own choices, and independence of persons;
b. Non-discrimination;
c. Full and effective participation and inclusion in society;
d. Respect for difference and acceptance of persons with disabilities as part of human diversity and humanity;
e. Equality of opportunity;
f. Accessibility;
g. Equality between men and women;
h. Respect for the evolving capacities of children with disabilities and respect for the right of children with disabilities to preserve their identities.

States Parties shall recognize that persons with disabilities *enjoy legal capacity on an equal basis* with others in all aspects of life.

States Parties shall take appropriate measures to provide access by persons with disabilities *to the support they may require in exercising their legal capacity*.

Chapter 9
The death penalty

This final short chapter on the death penalty serves as a reminder of how our attitudes with regard to what constitutes a human rights question change over time. For the drafters of the 18th century French and American Declarations, it was inconceivable that abolition of the death penalty could form part of their proclamations of rights. Even in 1945, there was no attempt at agreement on this issue among the 'united nations' that had fought the Second World War, and the 1948 Universal Declaration is obviously silent on this point. In modern times, about half the states in the world have formally abolished the death penalty, and actual use of the death penalty by the remainder is concentrated in a rather small number of states (see Box 39).

Some would question whether the death penalty should really be seen as a human rights issue. If treaties that outlaw the death penalty remain unsigned, and elected legislators choose to keep this form of punishment, then the grounds for saying that the death penalty is universally prohibited are thin. A simple response to these arguments is that the death penalty violates the right to life and is therefore wrong, and that, furthermore, if we are convinced that torture and inhuman punishment is absolutely prohibited then the ultimate irrevocable punishment of execution should also be prohibited at least as a form of inhuman

Box 39 Amnesty International, *Facts and Figures on the Death Penalty* (2014)

At least 607 executions were carried out worldwide, a decrease of almost 22 per cent compared with 2013. As in previous years, this figure does not include the number of people executed in China, where data on the death penalty is treated as a state secret.

Three countries—Iran, Iraq and Saudi Arabia—were responsible for 72 per cent of the 607 recorded executions. In Iran the authorities officially announced 289 executions, but hundreds more were carried out which were not officially acknowledged.

The following methods of executions were used: beheading (Saudi Arabia), hanging (Afghanistan, Bangladesh, Egypt, Iran, Iraq, Japan, Jordan, Malaysia, Pakistan, Palestine, Singapore, Sudan), lethal injection (China, USA, Viet Nam) and shooting (Belarus, China, Equatorial Guinea, North Korea, Palestine, Saudi Arabia, Somalia, Taiwan, UAE, Yemen).

At least 2,466 people in 55 countries are known to have been sentenced to death in 2014. This represents an increase of 28 per cent compared with 2013, when 1,925 death sentences were recorded in 57 countries. This increase was largely due to sharp spikes in death sentences in Egypt (from 109 in 2013 to 509 in 214) and Nigeria (from 141 in 2013 to 659 in 2014), both countries in which courts imposed mass sentences in some cases.

At least 19,094 people were believed to be under sentence of death worldwide at the end of 2014.

Mandatory death sentences continued to be imposed in Barbados, Iran, Malaysia, Pakistan, Singapore and Trinidad and Tobago. Mandatory death sentences are inconsistent with human rights protections because they do not allow any possibility of taking into account the defendant's personal circumstances or the circumstances of the particular offence.

More than two-thirds of the countries in the world have now abolished the death penalty in law or practice. As of 31 December 2014 the numbers were as follows:

Abolitionist for all crimes: 98

Abolitionist for ordinary crimes only: 7

Abolitionist in practice: 35

Total abolitionist in law or practice: 140

Retentionist: 58

punishment. For some organizations and for many individuals, there is no need to go beyond such logical conclusions.

Nevertheless, as just stated, governments after the Second World War were in no mood to abolish the death penalty in their human rights instruments protecting the right to life. The major human rights treaties were drafted with built-in limitations on the right to life; life could be taken by the state in the context of a judicially administered death penalty following a fair trial.

Let us see how the human rights treaties which allow for the death penalty have been interpreted to include procedural safeguards, limits on which crimes may be punished with a death sentence, and on who may be executed, as well as prohibitions on certain forms of execution.

The notion of a prohibition on *arbitrary* deprivation of life means that a death sentence may only be imposed following a fair trial with appropriate safeguards, including a fair hearing by an independent and impartial tribunal, the presumption of innocence, minimum guarantees for the defence, and review by a higher tribunal.

There is agreement among states that imposition of the death penalty be limited to the most serious crimes. The UN Human Rights Council's Special Rapporteur, Philip Alston, after a careful study of UN practice, concluded that 'the death penalty can only be imposed in cases where it can be shown that there was an intention to kill which resulted in the loss of life.'

Turning to the death penalty itself, we encounter the frontiers of what is, and what is not, accepted as a universal human right. Governments are divided about what is acceptable and what is not. But again, the idea that states, nations, peoples, or cultures are immutable is wrongheaded. South Africa abolished the death penalty as a result of its Constitutional Court's determination in 1995 that the death penalty violated the constitutional prohibition on cruel, inhuman, or degrading treatment. Other jurisdictions are continuing to assess when the death penalty may be unacceptable under their constitutional protections. The US Supreme Court held in 2002 that imposition of the death penalty for the 'mentally retarded' is prohibited as violating the constitutional prohibition on 'cruel and unusual punishments'. In 2005, the US Supreme Court held that it was unconstitutional for the death penalty to be imposed on those who were minors at the time of the offence. It is now therefore relatively uncontroversial that international norms prohibit the execution of juvenile offenders, the insane, and pregnant women. Some human rights texts also prohibit the execution of those over 70, those who have become insane, and nursing mothers.

The conditions surrounding execution have also given rise to an interesting set of prohibitions on *carrying out* the death penalty.

First, the prohibition of the death penalty has been interpreted to prevent states that have abolished the death penalty from extraditing or deporting individuals to face the death penalty elsewhere. Second, the anxiety of waiting for years to exhaust appeals is considered to amount to inhuman treatment (ironically, the solution is therefore said to be to speed up the process between trial and execution). Third, the method of execution could be found to constitute cruel and inhuman punishment; this can be significant where individuals about to be extradited can use procedures to prevent such extraditions on the grounds that this would lead to inhuman punishment. There have been challenges based on the cruelty of the drugs used in lethal injections (see Figure 15) and the European Union has banned exports of barbiturate anaesthetic agents as they can be used for executions. The difficulty in obtaining such drugs has led some US states to consider reintroducing the firing squad and the electric chair. For completeness we should mention perhaps that the same regulation bans the export of electric chairs, gallows, and guillotines (see Figure 15). Fourth, violations of fair trial guarantees can mean that any subsequent execution would be an arbitrary deprivation of life. Lastly, in a case concerning the sentencing to death of Abdullah Öcalan in Turkey, the European Court of Human Rights held that the anguish associated with a death sentence following an unfair trial 'by a court whose independence and impartiality were open to doubt' was to be considered inhuman treatment due to the anguish associated with the proceedings.

A death penalty trial may trigger extra procedural protection. Most recently the rules have been changed for the US Military Commission trying defendants in death penalty cases in Guantánamo. Since 2009 a defendant in such a case is supposed to be represented, to the greatest extent practicable, by at least one additional counsel who is learned in applicable law relating to death penalty cases, and who may be a civilian and compensated by the government. Moreover a death sentence requires the

14. '9/11 trial' in US Military Commission Guantánamo Bay Naval Base, from the front Khalid Shaikh Mohammad, Walid Muhammad Salih Mubarak bin Atash, Ramzi bin al Shibh, Ali Abdul Aziz Ali, Mustafa Ahmed Adam al Hawsawi, authorized sketch by Janet Hamlin 2014.

unanimous agreement of the panel of at least nine members, even if the defendant pleads guilty. These rules apply to the five defendants currently on trial in Guantánamo for plotting the attacks of September 11 in 2001 (see Figure 14).

With scientific advances concerning DNA testing and other methods of identification, there is greater confidence that only the guilty are being executed. This diminishes the force of the argument that the death penalty remains unacceptable due to the risk of executing an innocent human being. But of course such developments may also reinforce the case against the death penalty as scientific methods prove how the innocent have been executed or were about to be executed. Arguments concerning the cruelty of the death penalty can be

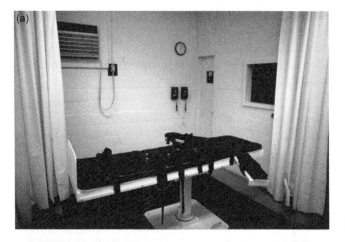

15. a. A lethal injection chamber in the US today, and b. the last public execution in France, which took place in 1937 in Versailles by guillotine. The guillotine was introduced in France as a humane method of execution in 1792 and was used until 1977.

met with new 'humane' ways to inflict death. But, ultimately, human rights principles ask us to see that the death penalty is an unnecessary interference with the right to life—as no immediate threat to another life is posed by the condemned human being.

Final remarks

The content of human rights is no longer solely determined through appeals to reason and natural law. Human rights texts have been negotiated and adopted at the national and international levels. These texts have a certain moral force based on the context of their adoption; and are legally significant because they are adopted by governments. Authoritarianism, deprivation, and slaughter are counterpoised with the promise of a future based on human rights.

But the promise of human rights remains unfulfilled around the world. Daily reports of violent abuse, injustice, and the denial of basic subsistence rights leave no room to doubt that we live in a world of human rights violations. Human rights reporting exposes the worst cases, but remains frustrated in the face of governments' failure to live up to their promise that they will step in to protect populations from genocide, war crimes, ethnic cleansing, and crimes against humanity. Human rights foreign policies stop far short of effective action in such crisis situations.

At another level, we have discussed the ways in which human rights bodies have developed human rights principles related to torture, the right to life, detention, freedom of expression, privacy, food, education, health, housing, work, and non-discrimination.

Many topics have admittedly been skated over or omitted. A bigger book would have to deal with the human rights arguments used to challenge threats to peace, poverty, austerity measures, environmental degradation, the impact of climate change, the rights of indigenous peoples, and the plight of refugees and displaced persons.

One aim of this book was to give the reader insights into how different human rights need to be considered one by one to appreciate the contours of their scope and the complexity of their implementation and interaction with other rights in any one situation. The language and logic of human rights should be seen as routes to arguing about claims and countervailing interests; human rights are not a closed book, but rather part of an ongoing conversation.

For human rights really to take hold, they will have to be understood and fully internalized. This means continuing to debate and develop the principles of human rights so that they meet people's needs and expectations. For human rights to have a greater impact, they have to appeal to people's imaginations and become properly part of their vocabulary. The vocabulary of human rights can help to formulate these demands. Expressing conflicts in terms of human rights language can reveal the competing interests at stake and suggest the appropriate principles and procedures for resolving the tension.

Human rights risk being seen, however, as alien, imposed, and instrumental for other ends unless more work is done to conquer the limited meaning they are often given. Those who insist on a narrow understanding seek to confine human rights to a historically based determination of specific governmental duties to refrain from infringing traditional liberties; a wider vision of human rights allows for consideration of the problems of hunger, poverty, and violence facing billions of people. Makau Matua, in his book *Human Rights: A Political and Cultural Critique*, argued in 2002:

> As currently constituted and deployed, the human rights movement will ultimately fail because it is perceived as an alien ideology in non-Western societies. The movement does not deeply resonate in the cultural fabrics of non-Western states, except among hypocritical elites steeped in Western ideas. In order ultimately to prevail, the human rights movement must be moored in the cultures of all peoples.

Similarly, Costas Douzinas, warned in 2000 in his book *The End of Human Rights: Critical Legal Thought at the Turn of the Century*

> Yet a theory of human rights which places all trust in governments, international institutions, judges and other centres of public or private power, including the inchoate values of a society, defies their *raison d'être*, which is precisely to defend people from those institutions and powers.

Even where the human rights movement has sought to expand the horizons of human rights protection, as with the campaign against violence against women, this may again be seen as imperfect. Some critics argue that human rights organizations may tend to generate a narrative that reinforces images of helpless victims oppressed by an alien culture; in turn, this could be said to continue imperialism by other means. These critics argue that the biggest challenge is to understand the origins of such inequality and violence, rather than simply categorizing violence against women as a question of human rights (see Box 40).

Human rights campaigners are learning that insisting on respect for human rights is not the only way to change the world. But insisting on human rights can be instrumental in ensuring that a wider variety of voices and suggestions are heard. Today there is a discernible move to take human rights work closer to the 'field',

Box 40 Ratna Kapur, *Erotic Justice: Law and the New Politics of Postcolonialism*

The class, cultural, religious and racial differences between women are collapsed under the category of gender through women's common experience of sexual violence and objectification by men. Differences between women are simply understood as cultural, without exploring or elaborating on how the cultural context was shaped and influenced in and through the colonial encounter—an encounter between the West and 'the Rest'. To miss this part of the argument is to present a narrative of women's exploitation and subordination that does not implicate the ways in which race, religion and imperial ambition constituted the vortex of knowledge that affords us a historically grounded and contextualized understanding of that experience.

the 'ground', or the 'people', and to concentrate not only on 'implementation of standards', but also on generating a culture of human rights where the concept of respect for human dignity is internalized.

It is remarkable that an oft-heard plea is that human rights should be less 'politicized'. This makes no sense. Human rights *are* political: they articulate the relationship between individuals and groups within a community and their relationship with others, particularly those with power and authority. That's national politics. If states set up a Human Rights Council at the UN, where governments discuss each other's records, that's international politics. The hope that governments will somehow set aside their economic and foreign policy interests to arrive at objective 'apolitical' assessments of the human rights behaviour of other states is vain indeed.

Individuals and groups will continue to feel empowered by the language of human rights and by the framework that has grown up to develop solidarity across the human rights movement for ensuring respect for these rights. When these claims are articulated as human rights demands, this often represents political participation rather than isolated individualism. The point here is to change things, including how human rights themselves are conceived. We have seen throughout this book that the protection of human rights is a dynamic process based on developing demands and changing views about what human rights require. The human rights movement is now concerned with global social justice. Human rights are vibrant not static.

We might finish by returning to the ways in which the expression 'human rights' has featured in literature. In his 1910 novel *Howards End*, E. M. Forster used the term 'human rights' to highlight the injustice of the way the unmarried pregnant Helen Schlegel is being treated by society, and the feelings of solidarity that the other heroine, Margaret, feels towards her sister Helen.

> Margaret's anger and terror increased every moment. How dare these men label her sister! What horrors lay ahead! What impertinences that shelter under the name of science! The pack was turning on Helen, to deny her human rights, and it seemed to Margaret that all Schlegels were threatened with her.

The passage illustrates how, then as now, human rights claims result simply from a sense of injustice and a feeling of solidarity.

Publisher's acknowledgements

We are grateful for permission to include the following copyright material in this book.

"Foreign funding of NGOs; Donors: keep out" *The Economist*, Sept 13, 2014 © The Economist Newspaper Limited, London (2014)

"Human rights; Stand up for your rights", *The Economist*, March 22, 2007 © The Economist Newspaper Limited, London (2007)

References

Many of the texts are available on the companion website for this Very Short Introduction <http://graduateinstitute.ch/clapham-humanrights>

Chapter 1: Looking at rights

Box 1: C. Grayling, 'We must seize power from Euro judges and return the phrase Human Rights to what it really should be—a symbol of the fight against oppression and brutality', *Daily Mail*, 3 October 2014; S. Marks, 'Backlash: The Undeclared War against Human Rights', *European Human Rights Law Review* (2014) at 323–4

W. A. Edmundson, *An Introduction to Rights* (Cambridge: Cambridge University Press, 2004), at 191

R. Falk, 'Rights', in *The Oxford Companion to Politics of the World*, 2nd edn, ed. J. Krieger (Oxford: Oxford University Press, 2001), at 734–5

Magna Carta (1215)

English Bill of Rights (1689)

J. Locke, *The Second Treatise of Government*, 1690 (New York: Macmillan, 1986), paras 6–8, 13, 221–2

J.-J. Rousseau, *The Social Contract, or Principles of Political Right*, anon. tr. 1791 (New York: Hafner, 1947), chs VII and VIII

T. Paine, *Rights of Man*, 1791 (Harmondsworth: Penguin, 1969), at 228, 69, 70

E. Burke, *Reflections on the Revolution in France*, ed. L. G. Mitchell (Oxford: Oxford University Press, 1993)

Box 2: M. Wollstonecraft, 'Dedication to Monsieur Talleyrand-Périgord', in *A Vindication of the Rights of Woman: With Strictures and Political and Moral Subjects* (1792)

Box 3: K. Marx, *On the Jewish Question*, 1843, excerpted in M. R. Ishay (ed.), *The Human Rights Reader: Major Political Essays, Speeches, and Documents from the Bible to the Present* (London: Routledge, 1997), at 196

J. Bentham, 'Anarchical Fallacies; being an examination of the Declaration of Rights issued during the French Revolution', Vol. 2, *The Works of Jeremy Bentham*, ed. J. Bowring (Edinburgh: William Tait, 1843)

A. Sen, *Development as Freedom* (New York: Knopf, 1999), 228–9

S. Howe, *Empire: A Very Short Introduction* (Oxford: Oxford University Press, 2002), 3

Box 4: Frédéric Mégret et al., *Human Dignity: A Special Focus on Vulnerable Groups* (Geneva: Geneva Academy, 2014), at vii

A. Gerwith, 'Are There Any Absolute Rights?', in *Theories of Rights*, ed. J. Waldron (Oxford: Oxford University Press, 1984), 91–109, at 108

J. Habermas, 'The Concept of Human Dignity and the Realistic Utopia of Human Rights', in *The Crisis of the European Union: A Response*, tr. C. Cronin (Cambridge: Polity, 2012), at 81 and 95

C. McCrudden, 'Human Dignity and Judicial Interpretation of Human Rights', *European Journal of International Law* 19 (4) (2008) 724

Vitner and Others v United Kingdom ECHR (life sentences), 9 July 2013, para 113

R. Rorty, 'Human Rights, Rationality, and Sentimentality', in *On Human Rights: The Oxford Amnesty Lectures*, ed. S. Shute and S. Hurley (Oxford: Oxford University Press, 1993), 118–19, 122

Box 5: M. Goodhart, 'Human Rights and the Politics of Contestation', in *Human Rights at the Crossroads*, ed. M. Goodale (Oxford: Oxford University Press, 2013), at 33

D. Kennedy, *The Dark Sides of Virtue: Reassessing International Humanitarianism* (Princeton, NJ: Princeton University Press, 2004) at 9

M. Kundera, *Immortality* (London: Faber and Faber, 1991), at 150–4

Box 6: Complaint to the UK National Contact Point under the Specific Instance Procedure of the OECD Guidelines for Multinational Enterprises: G4S plc, 27 August 2014

Chapter 2: Historical development and contemporary concerns

Box 7: ILO Report Profits and Poverty: The Economics of Forced Labour (2014) 7 and 13

Box 8: UN Report A/68/256, 2 August 2013 at para 29

Box 9: UN Report A/HRC/27/53, 22 July 2014, para 25

H. Lauterpacht, *An International Bill of the Rights of Man* (Oxford: Oxford University Press, 2013)

P. Alston, 'Conjuring Up New Human Rights: A Proposal for Quality Control', *American Journal of International Law* 78 (1984) 607–21

B. A. W. Simpson, *Human Rights and the End of Empire: Britain and the Genesis of the European Convention* (Oxford: Oxford University Press, 2004); and P. French, *Younghusband—The Last Great Imperial Adventurer* (London: Harper Perennial, 2004), at 296

'Final Act of the Havana Meeting of the American Institute of International Law', *American Journal of International Law*, Supplement: Official Documents 11 (2) (April 1917) 47–53

W. Wilson, 'Fourteen Points Speech', delivered in Joint Session, 8 January 1918

A. Cassese, *Human Rights in a Changing World* (Cambridge: Polity Press, 1990), at 17–18

P. G. Lauren, *The Evolution of International Human Rights: Visions Seen* (Philadelphia: University of Pennsylvania Press, 1998) at 135

N. Geras, *Crimes against Humanity: Birth of a Concept* (Manchester: Manchester University Press, 2011), at 4

L. Sohn, 'How American International Lawyers Prepared for the San Francisco Bill of Rights', *American Journal of International Law* 89 (1995) at 540, 543 (for details on Lapradelle)

'Déclaration des droits internationaux de l'homme', Resolution of the Institute of International Law (1927)

H. G. Wells, *The Rights of Man: or What Are We Fighting For?* (Harmondsworth: Penguin, 1940), 8–9, 11, 12, 31, 52

J. Dilloway, *Human Rights and World Order: Two Discourses for the H. G. Wells Society* (H. G. Wells Society, 1998). *The Declaration and Appendix to Wells's Phoenix: A Summary of the Inescapable Conditions of World Reorganisation* (London: Secker and Warburg, 1942) are both reproduced in this publication

F. D. Roosevelt, State of the Union Address 1941 (known as the 'Four Freedoms Speech'), delivered 6 January 1941

Trial of German Major War Criminals (Goering et al.), International
Military Tribunal (Nuremberg) Judgement and Sentence, 30
September and 1 October 1946' (London: HMSO, Cmd 6964), at
40, 41 (chapter 'Law of the Charter')

Joint Declaration of France, Great Britain and Russia, 24 May 1915

Box 11: R. Lemkin, 'Les actes constituant un danger général
(interétatique) considérés comme délits dedroit des gens',
Conference for the Unification of Penal Law, Madrid, 14–20
October 1933 (Pedone, Paris, 1934) [English insert attached to
offprint in Geneva Library]

Box 12: *Prosecutor v Radislav Krstić*, Case IT-98-33-A, ICTY
(Appeals Chamber), 19 April 2004

Box 13: Rome Statute of the International Criminal Court (1998)

Box 14: World Summit Outcome 2005 para 120

A. A. An-Na'im, 'Problems of Universal Cultural Legitimacy for
Human Rights', in *Human Rights in Africa: Cross-Cultural
Perspectives*, ed. A. A. An-Na'im and F. M. Deng (Washington, DC:
Brookings Institute, 1990); and A. A. An-Na'im, 'Toward a
Cross-Cultural Approach to Defining International Standards of
Human Rights: The Meaning of Cruel, Inhuman or Degrading
Treatment or Punishment', in *Human Rights in Cross-Cultural
Perspective*, ed. A. An-Na'im (Philadelphia: University of
Pennsylvania Press, 1992) at 20–1

B. Clifford, 'Introduction: Fighting for New Rights', in *The
International Struggle for New Human Rights*, ed. C. Bob
(Philadelphia: University of Pennsylvania Press, 2009), 1–13 at 4

Evans v United Kingdom, Judgment of the European Court of Human
Rights, 7 March 2006, at paras 46, 62, and 68

Chapter 3: Human rights foreign policy and the role of the United Nations

Box 15: P. Sieghart, *The Lawful Rights of Mankind: An Introduction
to the International Legal Code of Human Rights* (Oxford: Oxford
University Press, 1986) at vii

Box 16: S. Moyn, *The Last Utopia: Human Rights in History* (Boston,
MA: Harvard University Press, 2010), at 8

Box 17: Amnesty International, *Beginner's Guide to the Arms Trade
Treaty*, September 2014

Box 18: 'Foreign Funding of NGOs', *The Economist*, 13 September
2014

Box 19: Thematic UN special procedures

Report of the Commission on Human Rights (nuclear Commission), 21 May 1946, E/38/Rev.1

M. A. Glendon, *A World Made New: Eleanor Roosevelt and the Universal Declaration of Human Rights* (New York: Random House, 2002), at 113 and 170

Human Rights Council established by General Assembly Resolution A/RES/60/251 of 15 March 2006

Box 20: Human Rights Council Resolution A/HRC/RES/S-22/1

Box 21: UPR Info, 'Beyond Promises: The Impact of the UPR on the Ground' (2014), at 5 and 14

Human Rights Council Resolution on Sri Lanka, 11th Special Session, 2009

W. Kälin, 'Ritual and Ritualism at the Universal Periodic Review: A Preliminary Appraisal', in *Human Rights and the Universal Periodic Review: Rituals and Ritualism*, ed. H. Charlesworth and E. Larking (Cambridge: Cambridge University Press, 2014) 25–41 at 31–2

Statement of Mary Robinson, UN High Commissioner for Human Rights, on Situation in Chechnya, Russian Federation, 16 November 1999

New York Times, 'In Tour of Africa, US Pulls its Punches on Human Rights' (15 December 1997), 10

Special Procedures: Facts and Figures 2013

Chapter 4: Torture

Convention Against Torture and Other Cruel, Inhuman or Degrading Treatment or Punishment, entered into force 26 June 1987

Box 22: 'Opinion of Lord Hope of Craighead', in *A and Others v Secretary of State for the Home Department* [2005] UKHL 71, para 103

J. S. Bybee, Assistant Attorney-General, Memorandum for Alberto R. Gonzales, Counsel to the President, Re: Standards of Conduct for Interrogation under 18 U.S.C. §§2340–2340A, 1 August 2002

J. Yoo, Deputy Assistant Attorney-General, Memorandum for W. J. Haynes II, Re: Military Interrogation of Alien Unlawful Combatants Held Outside the United States, 14 March 2003

Senate Select Committee on Intelligence, *Study on the CIA Detention and Interrogation Program, Executive Summary and Conclusions, declassified revisions* 3 December 2014

Box 23: Guidance on Interviewing Detainees and the Passing and
Receipt of Information 2010

G. J. Tenet, P. J. Goss, M. V. Hayden, J. E. McLaughlin, and A. M. Calland,
'Ex-CIA Directors: Interrogations Saved Lives', *Wall Street Journal*
(10 December 2014)

*Public Committee Against Torture in Israel and Others v State of Israel
and Others*, Israel Supreme Court, 6 September 1999

Box 24: F. Jessberger, 'Bad Torture—Good Torture? What
International Criminal Lawyers May Learn from the Recent Trial
of Police Officers in Germany', *Journal of International Criminal
Justice* 3 (2005) 1059–73

S. Lukes, 'Liberal Democratic Torture', *British Journal of Political
Science* 36 (2005) at 13

Box 25: 'Opinion of Lord Rodger of Earlsferry', in *A and Others
[No. 2] v Secretary of State for the Home Department* [2005]
UKHL 71, para 132

Box 26: *Gäfgen v Germany*, European Court of Human Rights,
Judgment of 1 June 2010, para 187

Box 27: *Gäfgen v Germany*, Judgment of 1 June 2010, Joint Partly
Dissenting Opinion of Judges Rozakis, Tulkens, Jebens, Ziemele,
Bianku, and Power, para 9

Agiza v Sweden, Communication No. 233/2003, UN Doc. CAT/
C/34/D/233/2003 (2005)

'On Terrorists and Torturers'—Statement by UN High Commissioner
for Human Rights, Louise Arbour (7 December 2005)

Chapter 5: Deprivations of life and liberty

Basic Principles on the Use of Force and Firearms by Law
Enforcement Officials, Adopted by the Eighth United Nations
Congress on the Prevention of Crime and the Treatment of
Offenders, Havana, Cuba, 27 August to 7 September 1990

Box 28: 'White House Fact Sheet: Standards and Procedures for
the Use of Force in Counterterrorism Operations Outside the
United States and Areas of Active Hostilities', 23 May 2013;
Lawfulness of a Lethal Operation Directed Against a U.S.
Citizen Who Is a Senior Operational Leader of Al-Qa'ida or An
Associated Force. <http://www.cfr.org/terrorism-and-the-law/
department-justice-memo-lawfulness-lethal-operation-directed-
against-us-citizen-senior-operational-leader-al-qaida-associated-
force/p29925>

P. Alston, Report of the Special Rapporteur on Extrajudicial, Summary or Arbitrary Executions, 2010, para 33

Box 29: Rule 1: 'Principles of International Law on the Use of Force by States in Self-Defence', Chatham House (2005), at principle 5; Rules 2 and 3: 'ICRC Study on Customary International Humanitarian Law' (2005), at Rules 10 and 14

P. Benenson, 'The Forgotten Prisoners', *The Observer Weekend Review* (28 May 1961), at 21

Al-Nashiri v Poland [2014] European Court of Human Rights, Judgment of 24 July 2014, para 530

Box 30: *El-Masri v The former Yugoslav Republic of Macedonia* [2012] European Court of Human Rights, Judgment of 13 December 2012, paras 205 and 211

International Centre for Prison Studies, *World Prison Population Lists*, 10th edn

D. Kretzmer, 'Targeted Killing of Suspected Terrorists: Extra-Judicial Executions or Legitimate Means of Defence?', *European Journal of International Law* 16 (2005) 171–212

P. Halliday, *Habeas Corpus from England to Empire* (Cambridge, MA: Harvard University Press, 2010)

Chapter 6: Balancing rights—free speech and privacy

N. Mahfous, *Al-Ahram* (2 March 1989)

Box 31: 'Should Hate Speech be a Crime?', *New Internationalist* (December 2012), at 28–9

Report to the UN General Assembly 2014, A/69/397, paras 6 and 57

H. Charlesworth, C. Chinkin, and S. Wright, 'Feminist Approaches to International Law', *American Journal of International Law* 85 (4) (1991) 613–45

Hatton and Others v United Kingdom [2003] European Court of Human Rights Judgment of 8 July 2003, at 41

Box 32: *Ruusunen v Finland* European Court of Human Rights Judgment of 14 January 2014 at para 41–3

Google Spain Case ECJ, 13 May 2014, C-131/12, at para 81

The Economist, 'The Right to be Forgotten' (4 October 2014) at 61.

Chapter 7: Food, education, health, housing, and work

Box 33: *The Economist*, 'Stand Up for your Rights' (24 March 2007)

Box 34: C. R. Beitz, *The Idea of Human Rights* (Oxford: Oxford University Press, 2009), at 30–1

Soobramoney v Minister of Health, Republic of South Africa
Constitutional Court, Case CCT 32/97, 27 November 1997

Box 35: C. Gearty and V. Mantouvalou, *Debating Social Rights*
(Oxford: Hart, 2011) at 59

Kamayani Bali Mahabal, 'Enforcing the Right to Food in India—The
Impact of Social Activism', *ESR Review* (March 2004)

UN Committee on Economic, Social and Cultural Rights, *General
Comment 13 on the Right to Education*, 8 December 1999

Annual Reports of the UN Special Rapporteur on the Right to
Education

Campbell and Cosans v The United Kingdom ECtHR, Judgment of
25 February 1982

Committee on Economic, Social and Cultural Rights, *General
Comment 14 on the Right to the Highest Attainable Standard of
Health*, 11 August 2000

Decision of the General Council of the WTO on Implementation
of paragraph 6 of the Doha Declaration on the TRIPS
Agreement and Public Health, WT/L/540 and Corr.1, 1
September 2003

S. Leckie, 'The Right to Housing', in *Economic, Social and Cultural
Rights: A Textbook*, 2nd edn, ed. A. Eide, C. Krause, and A. Rosas
(The Hague: Nijhoff, 2001), at 150

Committee on Economic, Social and Cultural Rights, General
Comment No. 4 on the Right to Adequate Housing, 13 December
1991

Committee on Economic, Social and Cultural Rights, General
Comment No. 7 on the Right to Adequate Housing: Forced
Evictions, 20 May 1997

A. Eide, 'Adequate Standard of Living', in *International Human Rights
Law*, 2nd edn, ed. S. Shah, S. Sivakumaran, and D. Harris (Oxford:
Oxford University Press, 2014), at 204

OECD, Guidelines for Aid Agencies on Involuntary Displacement and
Resettlement in Development Projects, Paris 1992

World Bank Operational Policy 4.12: Involuntary Resettlement,
December 2001

Narmada Bachao Andolan v Union of India AIR (2000) SC 3751,
at 3827

Ogiek Community Order, African Court of Human and Peoples'
Rights, 15 March 2013

ILO Declaration on Fundamental Principles and Rights at Work, 86th
Session, Geneva, June 1998

J. G. Ruggie, *Just Business: Multinational Corporations and Human Rights* (New York: W.W. Norton, 2013), at xx–xxi

Committee on Economic, Social and Cultural Rights, General Comment No. 18 on the Right to Work, 6 February 2006

Chapter 8: Discrimination and equality

Human Rights Committee, General Comment 18 on Non-Discrimination, 10 November 1989

John K. Love et al. v Australia, Human Rights Committee, Communication No. 983/2001
U.N. Doc. CCPR/C/77/D/983/2001 (2003)

Minister of Home Affairs v Fourie, South African Constitutional Court (2005) para 60

The Economist, 'The Spread of Gay Rights', 19 October 2013

Eweida and others v UK [2013] ECtHR 37, Judgment of 15 January 2013

Christian Legal Society v Martinez, 561 U.S. 661 (2010), Judgment of 28 June 2010.

Bull v Hall [2013] UKSC 73 at para 48

Box 36: Human Dignity Trust (2014)

Committee on the Elimination of Racial Discrimination, General Recommendation 30 on Discrimination against Non-Citizens, 2004, para 35

Protocol to Prevent, Suppress and Punish Trafficking in Persons, Especially Women and Children, supplementing the United Nations Convention against Transnational Organized Crime, 2000

Secretary-General's Report on Conflict-Related Sexual Violence, 13 March 2014, S/2014/181

Box 37: Amnesty International, *It's in Our Hands: Stop Violence against Women*, 2004, AI Index: ACT 77/001/2004 at 11–12

Box 38: UN Convention on the Rights of Persons with Disabilities (2006) Articles 5(2), 2, 5(3), 3, 12(2)(3)

G. Quinn and C. O'Mahony, 'Disability and Human Rights: A New Field in the United Nations', in *International Protection of Human Rights: A Textbook*, 2nd edn, ed. C. Krause and M. Scheinin (Turku: Abo Akademi Institute for Human Rights, 2012), at 265–6

Chapter 9: The death penalty

Box 39: Amnesty International, *Facts and Figures on the Death Penalty 2014*, 3, 6, 7, 8, 64

Report of the Special Rapporteur on extrajudicial, summary or
arbitrary executions, Philip Alston, A/HRC/4/20, 29 January
2007, paras 39–53

The State v Makwanyane and Mchunu, Constitutional Court of the
Republic of South Africa, Case No. CCT/3/94, 6 June 1995

Atkins v Virginia 526 U.S. 304 (2002)

Roper v Simmons 543 U.S. 551 (2005)

Soering v United Kingdom [1989], ECtHR Judgment of 7 July 1989, 14

Öcalan v. Turkey [2005] ECtHR, Judgment of 12 May 2005, para 175

Military Commissions Act 2009, 10 US Code §949a and m

Commission Implementing Regulation (EU) No 1352/2011 of 20
December 2011 amending Council Regulation (EC) No 1236/2005
concerning trade in certain goods which could be used for capital
punishment, torture or other cruel, inhuman or degrading
treatment or punishment

Final remarks

M. Mutua, *Human Rights: A Political and Cultural Critique*
(Philadelphia, PA: Philadelphia University Press, 2002), p. 14.

C. Douzinas, *The End of Human Rights: Critical Legal Thought at the
Turn of the Century* (Oxford: Hart, 2000), 12

Box 40: R. Kapur, *Erotic Justice: Law and the New Politics of
Postcolonialism* (London: Glass House Press, 2005), 104

E. M. Forster, *Howards End*, 1910 (Harmondsworth: Penguin, 1989),
at 282

Further reading

The companion website for this Very Short Introduction can be found at <http://graduateinstitute.ch/clapham-humanrights>. On this website, you will find links to some of the texts we have mentioned, as well as a useful set of links to human rights sites.

The books listed below offer particular insights into the world of human rights. Those looking for other short introductions might like to consider O. Ball and Grady Paul, *The No-Nonsense Guide to Human Rights* (Oxford: New Internationalist, 2006). For a short introduction to any particular topic, see D. Forsythe (ed.), *Encyclopedia of Human Rights*, 5 volumes (New York: Oxford University Press, 2009). For academic essays on the foundations and principles, see D. Shelton (ed.), *The Oxford Handbook of International Human Rights Law* (Oxford: Oxford University Press, 2013).

Ways of looking at human rights

M. J. Perry's *The Idea of Human Rights: Four Inquiries* (Oxford: Oxford University Press, 1998) is a set of short essays which ask whether human rights are ineliminably religious, problematic, universal, and absolute. See also J. Griffin, *On Human Rights* (Oxford: Oxford University Press, 2008) for an attempt to determine an ethically substantive account of what are human rights based on a limited notion of 'personhood' or what is needed for human 'status'; and C. R. Betiz, *The Idea of Human Rights* (Oxford: Oxford University Press, 2009) who argues for an understanding of human rights as 'constitutive norms of an emergent global practice'. For a very thoughtful set of contemporary essays on dignity, see C. McCrudden (ed.), *Understanding Human Dignity* (Oxford: Oxford University Press, 2013).

For a critical examination of the ways in which historians see the emergence of the idea of human rights, one might look at S. Moyn's *The Last Utopia: Human Rights in History* (Cambridge, MA: Belknap Harvard, 2010) and his *Human Rights and the Uses of History* (London: Verso, 2014), he rejects many accounts and asks us to see human rights as we now understand them as taking on significance only after 1977 with the adoption of human rights by President Carter. Lynn Hunt's *Inventing Human Rights: A History* (New York: Norton, 2007) focuses on the 18th century and the influence of the novel in generating a sense of empathy. Micheline Ishay's *The History of Human Rights: From Ancient Times to the Globalization Era* (Berkeley: University of California Press, 2004) argues that religion contains humanistic elements that anticipated the modern conception of human rights and highlights the positive contribution of religion to the evolution of human rights. She also traces the precursors to rights thinking through different religious and other texts, including the Hammurabi Code from Babylon, the Hebrew Bible, the New Testament, and the Koran, and looks at Confucianism, Hinduism, and Buddhism. Ishay brings out the contribution of socialist ideas which developed against the background of 19th century industrialization. For a very useful analysis of the recent historiography of human rights and the debate over the genealogy of the human rights system, see P. Alston, 'Does the Past Matter? On the Origins of Human Rights', *Harvard Law Review* 126 (2013) 2043–81.

New empirical research on norm creation, diffusion, and institutionalization is brought together and critiqued in R. Goodman, D. Jinks, and A. K. Woods (eds), *Understanding Social Action, Promoting Human Rights* (Oxford: Oxford University Press, 2012).

For an enthusiastic historical overview of the people and ideas that have contributed to the human rights movement and the development of international human rights law, see Paul Lauren, *The Evolution of International Human Rights: Visions Seen*, 3rd edn (Philadelphia, PA: University of Pennsylvania Press, 2011); for reflections on the role of non-governmental organizations with particular insights from within Human Rights Watch, see A. Neier, *The International Human*

Rights Movement: A History (Princeton, NJ: Princeton University
Press, 2013) and J. Becker, *Campaigning for Justice: Human Rights
Advocacy in Practice* (Stanford: Stanford University Press, 2013).

Human rights protection

Adam Hoschschild's book, *King Leopold's Ghost: A Story of Greed,
Terror, and Heroism* (Boston: Houghton Miffin, 1998) provides
a fascinating and shocking insight into colonial rule and includes a
chapter on George Washington Williams (referred to in Chapter 2 for
his use of the expression 'crimes against humanity'). Samantha
Power's award-winning book recounts how the concept of genocide
was invented by Raphael Lemkin and how politicians in the United
States have failed to act in the face of genocide in the 20th century:
'A Problem from Hell': America and the Age of Genocide (New York:
HarperCollins, 2003). Power's book goes to the heart of the question
of US foreign policy and asks bigger questions. In her words: 'We
have all been bystanders to genocide. The crucial question is why.'
The impact of national criminal prosecutions for human rights
violations is described in detail in K. Sikkink, *The Justice Cascade:
How Human Rights Prosecutions are Changing World Politics*
(New York: Norton, 2011).

T. Risse, S. C. Ropp, and K. Sikkink (eds), *The Persistent Power of
Human Rights: From Commitment to Compliance* (Cambridge:
Cambridge University Press, 2013) contains studies on which
mechanisms are most effective in bringing about compliance with
human rights. The book usefully looks beyond the state and covers
compliance by multinational corporations, rebel groups and even
families (taking as a case study, female genital mutilation).

Foreign policy and international relations

A helpful introduction to human rights in international relations from
a political science perspective is David Forsythe's *Human Rights in
International Relations*, 3rd edn (Cambridge: Cambridge University
Press, 2012).

For an insider's account of the quest to create international criminal
tribunals, see D. Scheffer, *All the Missing Souls: A Personal History of
the War Crimes Tribunals* (Oxford: Princeton University Press, 2012).

For stimulating essays on the problems associated with the international criminal courts, see W. Schabas, *Unimaginable Atrocities: Justice, Politics, and Rights and the War Crimes Tribunals* (Oxford: Oxford University Press, 2012). Gerry Simpson lays out alternative ways of thinking about the law and politics in the field of war crimes law and exposes different political aspects of a number of well known war crimes trials: *Law, War and Crime: War Crimes Trials and the Reinvention of International Law* (Cambridge: Polity, 2008).

Rosa Feedman's engaging book offers a personal view on the workings of the Human Rights Council and highlights how some states use their power to avoid criticism at the UN Human Rights Council. She is sceptical about the idea of a World Court of Human Rights and suggests reinforcing regional organizations and their Courts. *Failing to Protect: the UN and the Politicisation of Human Rights* (London: Hurst, 2014). For the detail of the proposal for a World Court of Human Rights, see the commentary and consolidated statute contained in the 2011 Report of the Panel on Human Dignity *Protecting Human Dignity: An Agenda for Human Rights*.

Particular topics covered in this Very Short Introduction

The book *Torture Team* (Allen Lane: London, 2008) by Philippe Sands reveals how lawyers prepared the ground for decision-making that led to the torture and abuses carried out by agents of the United States in the wake of the 9/11 attack. This readable account contains first hand interviews with key players and asks questions about what we should expect from lawyers. For a variety of perspectives on the morality and legality of drone strikes, see C. Finkelstein, J. D. Ohlin, and A. A. Altman (eds), *Targeted Killings: Law and Morality in an Asymmetrical World* (Oxford: Oxford University Press, 2012). For a readable introduction to the politics of the creation and maintenance of the Military Commissions Guantánamo Bay, see J. Bravin, *The Terror Courts: Rough Justice at Guantanamo Bay* (New Haven: Yale University Press, 2013). For a complete overview of detention issues, see N. S. Rodley with M. Pollard, *The Treatment of Prisoners under International Law*, 3rd edn (Oxford: Oxford University Press, 2009).

An up to date look at privacy can be found in R. Wacks, *Privacy: A Very Short Introduction*, 2nd edn (Oxford: Oxford University Press, 2015).

For expert analysis of how rights to health and housing are implemented by courts in jurisdictions such as India, South Africa, and Canada, see *The Role of Judges in Implementing Economic, Social and Cultural Rights*, edited by Yash Ghai and Jill Cottrell (London: Interights, 2004); and for contemporary developments at the international level, see E. Riedel, G. Giacca, and C. Golay (eds), *Economic, Social and Cultural Rights in International Law* (Oxford: Oxford University Press, 2014). Sophisticated treatments of topics not covered in the present book include S. Humphreys (ed.), *Human Rights and Climate Change* (Cambridge: Cambridge University Press, 2010); T. Pogge, *World Poverty and Human Rights*, 2nd edn (Cambridge: Polity, 2008); S. J. Anaya, *International Human Rights and Indigenous Peoples* (New York: Aspen, 2009).

Further discussion regarding the rights discussed in this introduction can be found in an A–Z format in the *International Human Rights Lexicon* by Susan Marks and Andrew Clapham (Oxford: Oxford University Press, 2005).

Some theatre plays that take human rights violations in detention as their starting point include *The Jail Diary of Albie Sachs* (1981) by David Edgar, and *Death and the Maiden* (1991) by Ariel Dorfman, while the more recent play *Grounded* (2012) by George Brant considers the role of a drone operator. The radio play *A Pact of Silence* (2015) by Penny Woolcock dramatises the plight of the children of the disappeared in Argentina. We might also mention the films: *Hotel Rwanda* (2004) directed by Terry George, *Camp X Ray* (2014) directed by Peter Sattler, and *Good Kill* (2015) by Andrew Niccol.

Annex: The Universal Declaration of Human Rights

Preamble

Whereas recognition of the inherent dignity and of the equal and inalienable rights of all members of the human family is the foundation of freedom, justice and peace in the world,

Whereas disregard and contempt for human rights have resulted in barbarous acts which have outraged the conscience of mankind, and the advent of a world in which human beings shall enjoy freedom of speech and belief and freedom from fear and want has been proclaimed as the highest aspiration of the common people,

Whereas it is essential, if man is not to be compelled to have recourse, as a last resort, to rebellion against tyranny and oppression, that human rights should be protected by the rule of law,

Whereas it is essential to promote the development of friendly relations between nations,

Whereas the peoples of the United Nations have in the Charter reaffirmed their faith in fundamental human rights, in the dignity and worth of the human person and in the equal rights of men and women and have determined to promote social progress and better standards of life in larger freedom,

Whereas Member States have pledged themselves to achieve, in cooperation with the United Nations, the promotion of universal respect for and observance of human rights and fundamental freedoms,

Whereas a common understanding of these rights and freedoms is of the greatest importance for the full realization of this pledge,

Now, therefore,

The General Assembly

Proclaims this Universal Declaration of Human Rights as a common standard of achievement for all peoples and all nations, to the end that every individual and every organ of society, keeping this Declaration constantly in mind, shall strive by teaching and education to promote respect for these rights and freedoms and by progressive measures, national and international, to secure their universal and effective recognition and observance, both among the peoples of Member States themselves and among the peoples of territories under their jurisdiction.

Article 1

All human beings are born free and equal in dignity and rights. They are endowed with reason and conscience and should act towards one another in a spirit of brotherhood.

Article 2

Everyone is entitled to all the rights and freedoms set forth in this Declaration, without distinction of any kind, such as race, colour, sex, language, religion, political or other opinion, national or social origin, property, birth or other status.

Furthermore, no distinction shall be made on the basis of the political, jurisdictional or international status of the country or territory to which a person belongs, whether it be independent, trust, non-self-governing or under any other limitation of sovereignty.

Article 3

Everyone has the right to life, liberty and security of person.

Article 4

No one shall be held in slavery or servitude; slavery and the slave trade shall be prohibited in all their forms.

Article 5

No one shall be subjected to torture or to cruel, inhuman or degrading treatment or punishment.

Article 6

Everyone has the right to recognition everywhere as a person before the law.

Article 7

All are equal before the law and are entitled without any discrimination to equal protection of the law. All are entitled to equal protection against any discrimination in violation of this Declaration and against any incitement to such discrimination.

Article 8

Everyone has the right to an effective remedy by the competent national tribunals for acts violating the fundamental rights granted him by the constitution or by law.

Article 9

No one shall be subjected to arbitrary arrest, detention or exile.

Article 10

Everyone is entitled in full equality to a fair and public hearing by an independent and impartial tribunal, in the determination of his rights and obligations and of any criminal charge against him.

Article 11

1. Everyone charged with a penal offence has the right to be presumed innocent until proved guilty according to law in a public trial at which he has had all the guarantees necessary for his defence.

2. No one shall be held guilty of any penal offence on account of any act or omission which did not constitute a penal offence, under national or international law, at the time when it was committed. Nor shall a heavier penalty be imposed than the one that was applicable at the time the penal offence was committed.

Article 12

No one shall be subjected to arbitrary interference with his privacy, family, home or correspondence, nor to attacks upon his honour and reputation. Everyone has the right to the protection of the law against such interference or attacks.

Article 13

1. Everyone has the right to freedom of movement and residence within the borders of each State.

2. Everyone has the right to leave any country, including his own, and to return to his country.

Article 14

1. Everyone has the right to seek and to enjoy in other countries asylum from persecution.

2. This right may not be invoked in the case of prosecutions genuinely arising from non-political crimes or from acts contrary to the purposes and principles of the United Nations.

Article 15

1. Everyone has the right to a nationality.

2. No one shall be arbitrarily deprived of his nationality nor denied the right to change his nationality.

Article 16

1. Men and women of full age, without any limitation due to race, nationality or religion, have the right to marry and to found a family. They are entitled to equal rights as to marriage, during marriage and at its dissolution.

2. Marriage shall be entered into only with the free and full consent of the intending spouses.

3. The family is the natural and fundamental group unit of society and is entitled to protection by society and the State.

Article 17

1. Everyone has the right to own property alone as well as in association with others.

2. No one shall be arbitrarily deprived of his property.

Article 18

Everyone has the right to freedom of thought, conscience and religion; this right includes freedom to change his religion or belief, and freedom, either alone or in community with others and in public or private, to manifest his religion or belief in teaching, practice, worship and observance.

Article 19

Everyone has the right to freedom of opinion and expression; this right includes freedom to hold opinions without interference and to seek, receive and impart information and ideas through any media and regardless of frontiers.

Article 20

1. Everyone has the right to freedom of peaceful assembly and association.

2. No one may be compelled to belong to an association.

Article 21

1. Everyone has the right to take part in the government of his country, directly or through freely chosen representatives.

2. Everyone has the right to equal access to public service in his country.

3. The will of the people shall be the basis of the authority of government; this will shall be expressed in periodic and genuine elections which shall be by universal and equal suffrage and shall be held by secret vote or by equivalent free voting procedures.

Article 22

Everyone, as a member of society, has the right to social security and is entitled to realization, through national effort and international co-operation and in accordance with the organization and resources of each State, of the economic, social and cultural rights indispensable for his dignity and the free development of his personality.

Article 23

1. Everyone has the right to work, to free choice of employment, to just and favourable conditions of work and to protection against unemployment.

2. Everyone, without any discrimination, has the right to equal pay for equal work.

3. Everyone who works has the right to just and favourable remuneration ensuring for himself and his family an existence worthy of human dignity, and supplemented, if necessary, by other means of social protection.

4. Everyone has the right to form and to join trade unions for the protection of his interests.

Article 24

Everyone has the right to rest and leisure, including reasonable limitation of working hours and periodic holidays with pay.

Article 25

1. Everyone has the right to a standard of living adequate for the health and well-being of himself and of his family, including food, clothing, housing and medical care and necessary social services, and the right to security in the event of unemployment, sickness, disability, widowhood, old age or other lack of livelihood in circumstances beyond his control.

2. Motherhood and childhood are entitled to special care and assistance. All children, whether born in or out of wedlock, shall enjoy the same social protection.

Article 26

1. Everyone has the right to education. Education shall be free, at least in the elementary and fundamental stages. Elementary education shall be compulsory. Technical and professional education shall be made generally available and higher education shall be equally accessible to all on the basis of merit.

2. Education shall be directed to the full development of the human personality and to the strengthening of respect for human rights and fundamental freedoms. It shall promote understanding, tolerance and friendship among all nations, racial or religious groups, and shall further the activities of the United Nations for the maintenance of peace.

3. Parents have a prior right to choose the kind of education that shall be given to their children.

Article 27

1. Everyone has the right freely to participate in the cultural life of the community, to enjoy the arts and to share in scientific advancement and its benefits.

2. Everyone has the right to the protection of the moral and material interests resulting from any scientific, literary or artistic production of which he is the author.

Article 28

Everyone is entitled to a social and international order in which the rights and freedoms set forth in this Declaration can be fully realized.

Article 29

1. Everyone has duties to the community in which alone the free and full development of his personality is possible.

2. In the exercise of his rights and freedoms, everyone shall be subject only to such limitations as are determined by law solely for the purpose of securing due recognition and respect for the rights and freedoms of others and of meeting the just requirements of morality, public order and the general welfare in a democratic society.

3. These rights and freedoms may in no case be exercised contrary to the purposes and principles of the United Nations.

Article 30

Nothing in this Declaration may be interpreted as implying for any State, group or person any right to engage in any activity or to perform any act aimed at the destruction of any of the rights and freedoms set forth herein.

Index

A

Afghanistan 45, 85–6, 87, 107, 154
America *see* United States
Amnesty International 67, 84, 105, 149–50, 154–5
armed conflict 34, 41–2, 45–8, 57, 74, 100, 101–4, 134–5, 148
Argentina 73, 86, 181
Arms Trade Treaty 66–7
ASEAN (Association of South East Asian Nations) Declaration 60–3
asylum seekers 96–7

B

Bentham, Jeremy 10–12
Bill of Rights (1689) 6–7
Boko Harem 76, 117
Burke, Edmund 8–9

C

Canada 92
capital punishment *see* death penalty
children 56, 129, 136, 156
Chile 45, 60, 73, 85
China 67, 70, 154

civil and political rights 122, 125–6
corporal punishment 115, 129
crimes against humanity 38–49, 66, 83, 98, 134–5
culture 12, 17, 52, 55, 165

D

Dafur, Sudan 45
death penalty 153–8
   children and persons with mental disabilities 156
   deportation or extradition 157
   fair trials 155, 157–60
   life, right to 153, 155, 157–60
   'most serious crimes' 156
   torture and cruel, inhuman or degrading treatment 153, 157–60
   United States 156, 157–60
Declaration of the Rights of Man (France, 1789) 9, 23
deportation or extradition 57, 134, 157
detention 98–9, 104–9, 141
   fair trials 106
   Guantánamo Bay 158
   prisoners of conscience 106
   terrorists 101–3
   without charge 25–6

dignity xiii, 2, 5, 9, 14–17, 28, 37, 43, 51, 57, 90, 93, 103, 114, 116, 140–1, 143, 145, 152, 164
disability 57–8, 59, 80, 124, 127, 128, 139, 142, 145, 150–2
disappearances, enforced 57, 60, 73
discrimination
  affirmative action 150
  age 57, 142
  disabled persons 57, 150–2
  education 128
  European Union 139
  nationality 30–1, 146–8
  racial 30–1, 55, 72–3, 146–7
  religious 30, 142–5
  retirement ages 142
  same-sex marriage 142–5
  sexual 55–6, 128, 148
  sexual orientation 115, 142–5
  trafficking in humans 146–7
  Universal Declaration of Human Rights (1948) 33–4
  workers' rights 136, 139
drones 68, 100–4, 180, 181

E

economic, social, and cultural rights 51, 55, 125, 126, 130
education 127–9
employment *see* workers' rights and right to work
enforced disappearance 57
enforcement of human rights 52, 55–8, 125
Europe 53–5, 58–9
  see also European Union
European Court of Human Rights 53–5, 59, 107
European Union 65
  discrimination 139
  workers' rights 138–9

F

fair trials 106, 155, 157–60
food, right to 122, 123, 126–7
foreign policy of states 24, 63, 81
forgotten, right to be 98, 119–20
freedom of association 136
freedom of expression 49–50, 98, 110–14, 117–19, 123

G

gender 24, 46, 141–5, 148, 164; *see also* women
genocide 42–9, 60, 66, 83, 161
Germany 91, 94, 96
Gouge, Olympe de 10
Guantánamo Bay 25–6, 68, 157–8, 180

H

hate speech 17, 111–13
health, right to 125, 129–32
HIV/AIDS 58, 80, 131, 142
housing 123, 132–5
  displacement 134–5
  forced evictions 133
  security of tenure 133
  Universal Declaration of Human Rights (1948) 132
human dignity *see* dignity
Human Rights Act (1998) 2–5
Human Rights Watch 68, 70
humanitarian intervention 66–8
Hussein, Saddam 68

I

individualism 23, 30, 51, 165
inhuman or degrading treatment 56, 74, 85, 89, 92, 95, 129, 153, 156
International Bill of Rights 27, 54, 137

International Covenant on Civil
and Political Rights 53–4,
59, 72, 108–9, 113–4, 141–2
International Covenant on
Economic, Social and Cultural
Rights 53–4, 59, 72, 141–2
international crimes 38–49, 116,
134–5 *see also* crimes against
humanity; genocide;
war crimes
International Criminal
Tribunals 13, 38–49, 134–5
International Labour Organization
(ILO) 29, 30, 32, 135
Iraq 68, 77, 86–7
Islamic state 67–8, 76–7, 117
Israel 72, 90–1

K

Kundera, Milan 19–24, 104

L

League of Nations 30–5
Lemkin, Raphael 42–3, 48
life, right to 99–104, 153, 155,
157–60
Locke, John 7

M

Magna Carta 6, 23
Marx, Karl 12
migrant workers 56–7, 146
military intervention 67–8, 101
minorities, rights of 29–30, 32,
39, 51

N

national security 146
nationals, state's treatment of own
41, 63–5
natural law 5, 9–13, 161

natural rights 27
non-governmental
organizations 31, 49, 60,
70–2, 75–6, 79, 84–5, 104–6,
148, 178–9
non-state actors 18, 25, 32, 43, 57,
76–7, 112, 115–18, 120, 132,
136–7, 141, 143, 148
Nuremberg trials 38, 41–2

O

organ trafficking 33

P

Paine, Thomas 8–9
Pinochet, Augusto 60, 85
pollution 118
prisoners, rights of 3
privacy 114–120
freedom of expression 114,
117–19
international crimes 116
pollution 118
press 118
private and public sphere 115–17
right to be forgotten 119–20
surveillance 113–15
women, public and private
sphere and 117
private security companies 25
proportionality 99, 113–14, 120–1,
146, 156

R

racial discrimination 30–1, 55,
72–3, 146–7
reasonable accommodation 145,
151–2
regional organizations 3, 16, 52–3,
58–62, 65, 81, 138–9
religion 5, 30, 142–5
Roosevelt, Franklin 37

Rousseau, Jean-Jacques 7–8
Russia 21, 67, 81
Rwanda 43–4

S

self-defence, use of force in 99–100
Sen, Amartya 13
Serbia 44, 66
sexual orientation 58, 112, 115,
    142–5
sexual violence 46, 58, 116, 146–9,
    164
slavery, abolition of 8, 29, 31–3,
    53–4, 98, 135, 147;
    see also workers' rights
social clauses in trading
    agreements 136
social contract 7–8, 22, 51
South Africa 72, 105, 126,
    142–3, 156
Srebrenica 44–5
Sri Lanka 75, 78
Syria 67–8, 75–7

T

terrorists 90, 94, 95, 101–3
Tokyo International Military
    Tribunal 38, 44
torture 25–6, 56, 60, 68–9, 83–97
  CIA programme 106–7
  coercive interrogation 90
  confessions 83–5
  convention against 83, 85–6,
    93–5
  crimes against humanity 83
  cruel, inhuman or degrading
    treatment 56, 74, 85, 89, 92,
    95, 153, 157–60
  death penalty 153, 157–60
  diplomatic assurances 97
  evidence obtained by 93–5
  Guy Fawkes 83–4

necessity defence 91–2
state immunity 60
terrorism 90, 94, 95
United States 86–9, 93–6
war crimes 83
trade union rights 135, 138–9
trafficking of humans 32, 146–7
treaty bodies 58–61

U

United Kingdom 2–4, 88–89
United Nations
  Charter 38
  Commission on Human
    Rights 72–82
  expert mechanisms and special
    procedures 73, 80
  field operations 80, 82
  Human Rights Council 74–80,
    164
  Office of the High Commissioner
    for Human Rights 78, 81–2
  universal periodic review 75–80
United States
  death penalty 156, 157–60
  Declaration of Independence 9
  foreign policy 64, 68, 81
  self-defence, use of force in
    99–100
  terrorists 101–3
  torture 86–9, 93–6, 106–7
Universal Declaration of Human
    Rights (1948) 5, 27, 49–51
  detention 141
  discrimination 33–4
  food 127
  housing 132
  Socialist states 49–50
  standard of living 124
universal rights and standards 5–6,
    13, 156
universality of human
    rights 50–3

W

war crimes 38–49, 66, 83, 101, 134–5
water, right to 127, 133
Wells, H. G. 34–7
Western world 5, 13, 19–21, 23
  imposition of norms 70, 162–3
Williams, George Washington, 39–40, 179
Wollstonecraft, Mary 10–11
women 10–12
  culture 55–6, 165
  discrimination 55–6, 128, 148
  public and private sphere 117
  trafficking 147
  treaties 55–6
  violence against 18, 148–50, 163
workers' rights and right to work 29, 30, 135–9
  discrimination 136, 146
  forced labour 31–2, 33, 136, 137
  labour standards and working conditions 138
  migrant workers 56–7, 146
  trafficking 146–7
World Trade Organization (WTO) 135–6

Y

Yugoslavia, former 13, 44–5

SOCIAL MEDIA
Very Short Introduction

Join our community

www.oup.com/vsi

- Join us online at the official Very Short Introductions **Facebook** page.
- Access the thoughts and musings of our authors with our online **blog**.
- Sign up for our monthly **e-newsletter** to receive information on all new titles publishing that month.
- Browse the full range of Very Short Introductions online.
- Read **extracts** from the Introductions for free.
- Visit our library of **Reading Guides**. These guides, written by our expert authors will help you to question again, why you think what you think.
- If you are a teacher or lecturer you can order inspection copies quickly and simply via our website.